BREASTPLATE
and
BUCKSKIN

BREASTPLATE

and . .

A STORY OF EXPLORATION AND

. . . . BUCKSKIN

DISCOVERY IN THE AMERICAS

by

George E. Tait

Professor of Education
Ontario College of Education
University of Toronto

Illustrated by

Vernon Mould

Head of the Art Department
Upper Canada College, Toronto

McGRAW-HILL RYERSON LIMITED
Toronto   Montreal   New York   London   Sydney
Mexico   Panama   Johannesburg   Düsseldorf
Rio De Janeiro   Kuala Lumpur   New Delhi   Singapore

22 23 24 25   JD   5 4 3

ISBN 0-7700-3025-4

PRINTED AND BOUND IN CANADA

CONTENTS

I

THE CITIES OF GOLD

II

QUEST FOR THE ORIENT

III

FUR TRADERS AND BUSHRANGERS

IV

NORTHWEST AND NORTH

V

ROMANCE OF THE PACIFIC COAST

VI

CABINS IN THE WILDERNESS

TO THE BOYS AND GIRLS WHO READ
THIS BOOK

*From time to time you will find words which may
be new to you underlined like this. So that you
may learn what they mean, you will find these words
listed under "Things to Know" on pages 225 to 234
with a full explanation.*

THE DAWN OF AMERICAN DISCOVERY—
AN INTRODUCTION

Breastplate and Buckskin is the story of exploration and discovery in the Americas—the story of an exciting period that began centuries ago in the heart of Europe and Asia. It is a story crowded with the vivid figures of men who won a New World beyond the unknown seas. Shut your eyes and you can see them. Listen, and you can hear them . . . the creak of anchor chains . . . the tramp of feet . . . the dip of paddles . . . the rattle of musketry . . . the fierce, wild warwhoops . . . and then . . . the sharp ring of axes . . . the soft lowing of cattle, and . . . the sweet lullabies of pioneer women.

I

To understand it all we must go back to the Middle Ages when long camel caravans plodded slowly from China across Afghanistan, over the Euphrates River to Palestine, or north by way of Armenia to Constantinople. On the backs of the shuffling camels were packed sweet-smelling bales of spices, ginger, tea, sugar, dyes, silks, cottons and drugs. Month after

1

month, year after year, the caravans swayed forward over hot plains, cold mountain passes and steep rocky trails. On the longest routes it sometimes took as many as six years for a caravan to make its way from the Mediterranean to China and back home again. For the traders it was a tedious and dangerous life, but the rewards were high!

At Mediterranean seaports the merchants met the dusty caravans and bargained eagerly for the precious loads of the camels. Then the goods were stowed away on Venetian vessels and moved to the seaports of Western Europe. There was such a brisk demand for the ships' rich cargoes that the wily merchants had no difficulty in selling their Eastern merchandise at fabulous prices.

The Crusades or Holy Wars caused an even greater interest in the wonderful goods of the Orient. When the Holy Land was captured by the Mohammedans, there was deep feeling among the Christians of Europe. Church leaders demanded that armies be raised and sent to Palestine. In 1096 the first expedition of Crusaders left Europe with the purpose of driving the infidels from the land where Christ lived and taught. For the next two hundred years the struggle continued its futile course. During the battles and sieges of the long campaigns hundreds of knights from Western Europe, wearing heavy armour marked with the big red cross, lost their lives. Jerusalem, it is true, was captured and held for a short time, but in the end the Mohammedans swept the Crusaders from the Holy Land.

While the men from Western Europe were in the Holy Land, they had the opportunity of seeing the amazing things brought from the Far East. Here were products and articles of which they had never dreamed: soft delicate fabrics, precious stones, delicious tropical fruits, exotic perfumes, shining glass, strange food and gunpowder. To western eyes these were treasures much finer and more exquisite than those

THE MEDITERRANEAN WORLD

produced in their own countries. And when the Crusaders went home carrying samples of these goods, all Europe realized the wealth of the Orient.

Western Europe was never the same after the Crusades. So many knights and noblemen had been killed that their loss affected the old ways of life. The nobles lost much of their power, many big estates disappeared, kings became more powerful, large towns sprang up, and a middle class of merchants appeared. With increasing prosperity coming to the countries of Europe, trade between East and West continued to expand.

II

An event in 1453, however, brought swift change to trading practices. During that year the Turks moved westward and captured the important trading seaport of Constantinople. This was a serious blow to trade because the Turks had no love for the peoples of Western Europe. The conquerors of Constantinople simply cut the trade routes from the Orient, almost stopping the flow of eastern goods. It is true that a trickle of trade continued, but it was not nearly enough to satisfy the demands of Europe.

The European countries were forced into making a choice between fighting the Turks and finding new trade routes to India and China. The Crusades had been a bitter lesson, so that no one was anxious to start a new war. Even before the capture of Constantinople by the Turks, European geographers and sailors had been thinking that unknown sea routes might lie out beyond the explored waters that surrounded the continent.

Centuries before this time bold navigators of Carthage and Greece had tried to sail around the continent of Africa, but their voyages had met with little success. Their ships had been small and their knowledge of navigation imperfect. By the fifteenth century Europeans were building larger vessels and were using the compass which had been invented in China. They had, too, the astrolabe, an instrument which enabled them to reckon their sailing position in terms of latitude and longitude.

The Portuguese, who had long been skilful mariners, took a special interest in the African sea route. They pushed farther and farther southward along the coast of the continent. By 1418 they had reached Madeira, and thirty years later Vasco da Gama completed an adventurous voyage about Africa and succeeded in reaching India. Here was a route by which trading vessels could sail directly from Europe to the East! During the following years the Portuguese mariners sent their vessels around the Cape of Good Hope to the shores of India, and after many months they returned to Lisbon with rich cargoes. With this wealth pouring into the country, Portugal became a leading trading nation in Europe.

While the Europeans had known for centuries that an African route existed, they had little knowledge of what lay across the waters of the Atlantic. There were, of course, many myths and legends. It was said that the great ocean could never be crossed because great whirlpools, giant sea serpents, even the ends of the earth lay beyond the horizon.

Today we know that about the year 1000 the Norsemen reached America from their settlements in Greenland and Iceland, and that groups of Irish and Scottish sea rovers may have come to the shores of our country. These voyages, however, were not well-known in Europe of the fifteenth century. It is improbable that Christopher Columbus ever heard of the Norse explorations and the accidental discovery of a new continent.

Columbus was the first mariner to sail under the Spanish flag in search of western sea routes. A tall grey-haired man of great courage and determination, he believed that the world was round and that the East could be reached by sailing westward across the Atlantic. This idea was not new. Many European scholars held the same belief, but Columbus was the first man willing to test the theory by sailing westward in search of India and China.

The Italian mariner made three voyages to America without suspecting that he had re-discovered a vast new world of two massive continents, a new world that offered greater opportunities than the ancient world of the Orient. Although Columbus was not the first European to reach America, his was the most important voyage of discovery, for it awakened Europe to the fact that a new and glorious world lay to the west.

III

The successes of Portugal and Spain in sea exploration caused some jealousy in England. King Henry VII decided that his nation too should be looking after her trading interests. In 1496, just four years after the first voyage of Columbus, he sent off an expedition under an Italian seaman, John Cabot. Twice this daring navigator reached the eastern shores of America, and like Columbus, he believed that he was in the outer fringes of the Orient. His voyages appeared to be failures at the time, for his ships brought back none of the luxuries of the Indies. The English merchants were keenly disappointed in his cargoes of fish and furs. Nevertheless, we know today that Cabot's explorations were important: they opened the great cod fisheries of the Grand Banks and they gave England a sound claim for land in America.

It would have been very natural if the New World had been named Columbia, Cabotana, Vikingland or some such name in honour of the first explorers, but this was not to be. Through the mistake of a German scholar another name came into being. Shortly after the voyages of Columbus an Italian merchant, Amerigo Vespucci, made two trips to South America on board Portuguese and Spanish sailing vessels. He wrote splendid letters of his travels, and these were circulated in Europe before the written accounts of Columbus. Amerigo Vespucci wrote glowingly of the New World he had seen. A German geographer, thinking that the Italian merchant was the true discoverer, suggested that the new lands be called *America*. The name was readily accepted, and retained even after the error was revealed. As time went by, the two continents of the New World came to be known as the "Americas."

THE CITIES OF GOLD

I

1 PONCE DE LEON

The Spaniards were quick to follow up the discoveries of Christopher Columbus, forming a number of active colonies in the West Indies. Men cleared land, grew crops of sugar cane, worked gold mines, and cut the beautiful dyewood trees. Spanish seamen sailed their ships among the islands, exploring the green shores or searching for legendary treasure. Crafty slave hunters, without the King's permission, slid stealthily along the coast watching for unwary natives. Not all voyages were recorded, for many captains had good reason to keep their travels as close-guarded secrets. There has come down to us, however, the interesting story of famous voyages to Florida.

Dazzling sunlight poured over the tops of palm trees on a harbour in Puerto Rico. Two Spanish lads, Juan and Carlos, sat in the shade talking lazily in low tones. Their eyes roved the waters and came to rest on three graceful ships anchored at the docks.

Juan yawned and asked curiously, "Carlos, who owns those ships?"

"Ponce de Leon," replied Carlos promptly.

Juan sat up straight. "You mean Juan Ponce de Leon—the Indian fighter—the man who was governor of Puerto Rico?"

"That's right," said Carlos. "People say that he is making an expedition in search of the Fountain of Youth."

Juan laughed. "Fountain of Youth! Don't be silly! Who believes that old Indian tale? Why it's been a joke for nearly twenty years! It's just stupid to think that there is a spring whose waters give youth to old men and old women."

Carlos frowned. "Don't be so sure. The Indians say there is such a fountain, and I know that Ponce de Leon is out to find it."

Juan laughed again. "Look, Carlos," he said. "Ponce de Leon knows this part of the world—he was with Columbus on the second voyage—he fought in the Indian campaigns—he's a tough soldier and a practical man, not one to go off chasing rainbows. If he is hunting for something it will be gold, land or even slaves."

Today we are not certain as to whether Juan or Carlos was correct; possibly both were partly right in their thoughts about the Spanish expedition. At any rate, Ponce de Leon did leave Puerto Rico with three ships in March 1513, and sailed through the West Indies in a northwesterly direction. His company was composed of hardy, experienced soldiers and sailors, but he took with him no priests, doctors nor trained geographers. His ships were very much like those of Christopher Columbus —tall vessels that travelled fairly well. In thirty days he had sailed eleven hundred miles from Puerto Rico to the latitude of 30.08 degrees up the east coast to a point a few miles north of the present city of St. Augustine. After the heat and close quarters of the voyage, the green shores appeared cool and inviting, so that the men splashed ashore in good spirits. In a short ceremony Ponce de Leon claimed the new land for Spain, and named it *Pascua Florida,* perhaps because of the flowers he saw everywhere.

After a short stay he decided to continue his explorations, and ordered his ships to turn southward along the Florida coast. As the ships entered the flow of the Gulf Stream the helmsmen tugged at their wheels, fighting against the pull of the current that slowed the speed of the vessels. Having reached the very tip of the peninsula, the expedition turned westward into the Gulf of Mexico and finally reached the Tortuga Islands. Then the ships swung northward along the

After a voyage of thirty days from Puerto Rico, Ponce de Leon was glad to land on the green shores of Florida. He and his men rowed ashore to a sandy beach backed by tall palm trees.

west coast of Florida and kept on until they reached a broad inlet, probably Tampa Bay, where anchors were dropped into the warm waters. The vessels had been sailing sluggishly, so Ponce de Leon decided to make repairs before proceeding further. The hull of the largest vessel had to be scraped thoroughly, for it was heavy with clinging sea plants and encrusted with rough barnacles. While the seamen scraped and made repairs, Indians appeared and began trading in skins, food and small articles of gold. To the surprise of the visitors one of these natives spoke Spanish words which were quite understandable, an astonishing fact in a country which Ponce de Leon believed had never before been reached by his countrymen. How this Indian learned to speak Spanish is not fully understood, but it is possible that he may have come to Florida from Haiti, a thousand miles away!

The Indians of the region were Timucans, a tall, strong people whose skins were light brown in colour. Their first friendliness toward the visiting seamen wore off rapidly, for they became hostile and threatened the Spanish ships. Moving swiftly in canoes and wading in the water they tried to drag the vessels ashore by pulling on the heavy anchor chains.

Ponce de Leon took in the situation at a glance, and shouted commands. "Smash up those canoes. Get men aloft with crossbows!"

One of the smaller Spanish vessels ploughed through the canoes, knocking shouting Indians into the water, while crossbows twanged from the rigging and high decks.

The natives were beaten back, and they howled defiance from the shore. Ponce de Leon ordered the ships moved to another anchorage, but still they were not safe, for several days later a second attack was launched. It was a fierce engagement that lasted for hours, and only with cannon could the sweating crews throw back the determined assault of the Timucans.

Three months after starting the voyage the Spanish ships set sail for home, and there was good reason for leaving: the vessels were worm-eaten and waterlogged; food supplies were running low. At the Tortuga Islands the seamen were able to secure some additional meat in the form of turtles, manatee and sea birds. Then on they went, southward toward Cuba, eastward to the Bahamas and on to Puerto Rico.

If Ponce de Leon searched for a Fountain of Youth, he certainly did not find one. He was well satisfied with the results of the voyage for he had discovered a spacious land of good soil and big trees. The only disadvantage of the new territory appeared to be the warlike spirit of the big Timucans.

To conquer such a land, he realized, would not be a simple matter.

Pleasant memories of lovely Florida remained in his mind, and eight years later he returned to the west coast, prepared to establish a colony near Tampa Bay. But as he landed, death watched from the mangroves—a long slim shaft whispered through the air and struck with a soft thud. Ponce de Leon collapsed on the beach. The Spanish soldier who had killed so many Indians was himself destroyed by a Timucan arrow.

It has often been said that Ponce de Leon was the discoverer of Florida, but this is not likely. Some people believe that John Cabot may have reached the northern part of Florida during his second voyage. There is also some reason to think that Amerigo Vespucci may have landed on the same coast. Then, too, it is quite possible that Spanish pirates or slave hunters made secret voyages there years before the time of Ponce de Leon.

Whether or not Ponce de Leon was the first to land in Florida is not important; his voyages caused Spanish eyes to turn toward the green peninsula. Between the years 1513 and 1549 no less than nine recorded expeditions reached the shores near Tampa Bay, and no one knows how many ships raided the coast for Indian slaves.

2   THE AZTEC PEOPLE

At the time when Columbus, Cabot and Da Gama were making their great sea voyages, there lived in the land of Mexico an Indian people whose way of life was truly amazing.

I

In the early stages of their history the Aztecs were an ordinary tribe of hunters who moved into the lake country where Mexico city now stands. Here they found other Indian peoples who were more civilized than they. As time went on, they learned many of the arts practised by their neighbours, but they were unable to live in peace with them. Defeated in battle by the Alcolhuacans, the Aztecs withdrew to islands in a lake and there they established themselves.

Surrounded by enemies, the Aztecs were forced to live as best they could on the small territory they controlled. The islands did not provide enough land for growing the vegetables and grains that they required, so the Aztec farmers devised a clever method of increasing their garden areas. First they built large rectangular rafts from reeds and sticks. Then the rafts were piled with soft mud from the lake, and in this soil seeds were planted. Thus it was that the famous Floating

Gardens were developed. After many crops had been reaped, the rafts became heavy and solid with masses of roots, and eventually became anchored to the bottom of the lake. More and more rafts were built until only narrow canals remained between them. Remnants of the old Floating Gardens still remain on the outskirts of Mexico city and these provide one of the greatest tourist attractions on this continent. Descendants of the Aztec people still pole their canoes along narrow canals bordered by tall trees and gorgeous flower gardens.

The tribe grew in numbers and became more powerful as the centuries went by. The Aztecs built up armies and succeeded in conquering many of the neighbouring people. When no wars were in progress, they invented pretexts for raids on other Indians. So great was their success that by the middle of the fifteenth century they controlled an empire that covered most of southern Mexico, much of the eastern coast and even part of Guatemala. The conquered tribes were forced to pay taxes, with the result that a constant stream of wealth poured into the treasury of the Aztec Emperor.

The Aztecs had progressed far from their earlier state of humble hunters and fishermen. They became skilled farmers who grew crops of corn, sweet potatoes, beans, peppers, tobacco, cotton, hemp, rubber, chocolate, and a great variety of flowers. It is a remarkable fact too that they raised turkeys in great numbers and sometimes used them as a form of money.

Not all the Aztecs were farmers, for many engaged in the crafts. There were silversmiths and goldsmiths, woodcarvers and sculptors, jewellers and feather-workers, spinners and weavers, tailors and milliners, sandal-makers and basket weavers, potters and tanners.

The clothing of the Aztecs was well made and beautifully designed. Men wore breech-cloths, capes and sandals. The noblemen, of course, wore more elaborate costumes of fine materials which were embroidered with intricate patterns.

Women wore short skirts and blouses decorated in accordance
with their station in life.

Among the most interesting costumes were those worn by
the warriors. Armour made from quilted cotton material was
very much in favour among the soldiers and officers. Such
armour, an inch in thickness, was soaked in salt water to give
it further strength and stiffness. These protective garments
were completely covered by feathers and bands of silver and
gold. The feathers not only provided additional protection,
but were used to distinguish groups of soldiers. Companies of
troops used their own particular colours in the feathered
coverings. So covered with feathers were some of the warriors,
that they resembled great tropical birds. Aztec warriors of
note were permitted to wear magnificent headdresses which
appeared to be part mask and part helmet. These were made
in fanciful shapes often representing animals and birds such
as the jaguar, the snake and the eagle. Very important leaders
wore long flowing capes and tall headdresses of green feathers.

The skill and the intelligence of the Aztecs were well
displayed in their buildings. It is true that the houses of the
common people were simple affairs of mud and thatch, but
the homes of the nobles were gracious places made from adobe
brick or cut stone. Government buildings too were large stone
structures, well planned and skilfully constructed. Great
engineering feats were accomplished in the building of roads,
bridges and dikes about the capital city of Mexico. Stone
causeways miles in length were built between the islands and
points along the mainland coast. An important modern high-
way still follows the route of an old Aztec causeway.

II

The most honoured positions in Aztec life were either
military or religious, so that it was only natural that young

The Aztec markets were exciting places filled with colour. Here were sold corn, potatoes, beans, cotton, chocolate, turkeys, flowers, baskets, pottery, clothing and many other things.

boys should hope to become either soldiers or priests. When old enough, boys were taken into schools where work was hard and discipline severe. There were some schools for girls too, but training was not so rigid.

Government of the Aztecs was a very systematic arrangement. There were local councils for governing small groups called *kins,* and larger councils for controlling the affairs of the cities. Over all stood a powerful emperor and a body of advisers. Each of the conquered provinces was controlled by a governor. The laws of the land were very strict and regular courts were held before magistrates. Murderers were put to death, robbers were whipped or imprisoned, slanderers had their lips cut off. Wealthy and poor people were treated alike, and there was no such thing as a criminal avoiding justice simply because he was the member of a noble family.

Religion was most important to these people. It even might be said that Aztec life centred about the numerous gods that they worshipped. Almost every day in the year was connected with some god or goddess, who must be worshipped and appeased by some form of sacrifice. Priests were powerful men who had authority in both religious and civil matters. Life in the temples was a busy one, for incense was burned many times a day before the images of gods, and offerings of flowers, food, clothing and other gifts were placed on the altars.

Unfortunately not all the religious ceremonies were as innocent as these. Blood was considered the highest and most important offering to be placed at the feet of the gods. Not only birds and animals were killed on the altars, but humans by the thousands were sacrificed in the most cruel manner. Old records tell of these hideous ceremonies where men and women were dragged up the long stairs of the pyramidal temples. Each captive in turn was seized by a group of priests and placed across a low sacrificial stone. Then one of the priests, dressed in red, plunged a knife into the breast of the victim, tore out the heart and held it up to the sun before laying it on the altars. The torn bodies were thrown down the long stairs of the pyramid. Such spectacles took place several times a year before great masses of people who watched, fascinated by the gory work of the priests.

In spite of their attachment to the rites of human sacrifice, the Aztecs held other celebrations which were more pleasant in form. At such times dancing, singing and offering of fruits and flowers were important events. A great love of flowers existed among the people, and indeed this trait may still be seen among the Mexicans. They were fond, too, of sports, taking much interest in tumbling, juggling and a ball game called *tlachtli*. The Aztec capital boasted a magnificent zoo which contained many animals, snakes and all the known birds of the country.

By the year 1500 the Aztec people had reached the height of their power. Their civilization was unsurpassed in the Americas and their military triumphs had built up a great and wealthy empire. Such was their prosperous condition when the Spanish arrived in the New World.

3 CORTÉS IN MEXICO

As Spanish power spread in America, romantic stories of life in the colonies were carried back to Europe. Young men in Spain, hearing these vivid tales, became very anxious to enter the service of the government as soldiers, sailors and adventurers.

I

A handsome young Spaniard approached his father and hesitated nervously before speaking.

"Father," he said, "I am through with college!"

The Spanish gentleman straightened up stiffly, and a look of swift anger crossed his face. "Through with college! That's ridiculous, Hernando! You can't mean it!"

Hernando looked soberly at his parent. "But I do mean it," he said. "You know that I will never make a good lawyer."

"My boy, you must get a good education. You must amount to something!"

Hernando cleared his throat, but went on eagerly. "I want to join the army, and go to the colonies. In the New World I can fight Indians, conquer new lands, make a fortune. There is no adventure left in Spain!"

His father's anger died away, and a sad expression gathered in his face. "I'm sorry you feel that way, Hernando, but after all, you are a man now—I won't stop you, if you wish to go."

So Hernando Cortés, at nineteen years of age, went off to America with dreams of wealth and adventure racing through his mind. Much to his disgust when he arrived, he was given a grant of land, and it was suggested that he grow sugar cane. This was scarcely the romantic career he had planned for himself! His chance for exciting action came, however, when the Spaniards invaded the island of Cuba. In this campaign he proved himself so fearless that his bravery won the respect of his commanding officer. As a result he was promoted and gained the attention of the new governor of Cuba.

The future appeared very promising, but the restless Cortés soon found himself in difficulties. To begin with, he refused to marry a beautiful girl of noble family. Then he quarrelled with the governor and was put in prison. This was a desperate situation for the young Spaniard, but eventually he regained the favour of the governor and married the senorita. Settling down to a quieter life in Cuba, he became a wealthy man through his plantations and mines. This life was very pleasant, but it was not entirely to his satisfaction. He still longed for excitement and action.

Events still unknown to the young Spaniard were taking place which were to give him more adventure than he hoped for. Spanish ships on a slave-hunting expedition had found unbelievable wealth in Mexico! When this startling news reached the colonies, there was great excitement among the people. The governor of Cuba decided to send a fleet of ships to this amazing country of gold and precious stones. Cortés to his own unbounded delight was chosen to lead the expedition. Here was his great chance! He was commanded to trade with the Indians, to spread Christianity, to explore the coast, and to study the products, people and general nature

Cortés landed on the Mexican coast near the Vanderas River.

of Mexico. Quickly he prepared for the great adventure, using his own money to secure ships, food stores, men and military equipment.

Before he was fully prepared for the voyage, Cortés was alarmed to hear that the governor had changed his mind about the leadership of the expedition. Determined to sail at all costs, he assembled his men on six ships and gave orders to cast off. The angry Governor arrived at the harbour just as the ships drew away from shore! Cortés knew that if the expedition proved a failure, he well might suffer death as a penalty.

Cortés reached the eastern shores of Mexico on March 4, 1519, and put ashore near the Vanderas River where the city of Vera Cruz now stands. Indians flocked to see the strangers, bringing gifts of flowers, fruits, vegetables and small gold ornaments. Cortés and his soldiers were greatly impressed by the fine appearance of the people, their excellent clothing and their polite manners. These were indeed the most civilized Indians they had yet seen.

The next day the governor of the district arrived and was received warmly by the Spaniards. Cortés informed this Aztec official that the white men who had just arrived on the shores of Mexico were subjects of the mightiest king on earth, a great monarch who lived far across the sea in Spain. They wished, Cortés said, to bring greetings to the mighty Emperor of the Aztec people. With some scorn in his voice, the Governor expressed surprise that the Spanish King could be as great as his own Emperor, Montezuma. The Emperor could only be seen, he said, if royal permission were to be granted.

In order to impress the Aztec governor, Cortés ordered his cavalrymen to ride their horses at the gallop across the beach while trumpets sounded and cannon balls whistled through the trees. All of this was faithfully recorded by skilful Aztec artists who drew detailed pictures of the Spaniards, the horses, the ships and the cannon. This was the famous picture-writing of the Aztec people, and those particular drawings were being prepared for the eyes of Montezuma.

II

After a week's time the Spaniards were startled by the appearance of several Aztec nobles. They were accompanied by a hundred slaves carrying gifts from the Emperor: helmets, bracelets, sandals, fans, precious stones, beautiful robes, feathered headdresses, yards of fine cottons and two round plates of silver and gold "as large as carriage wheels." Cortés and his men gasped in astonishment; their faces shone with greed.

Cortés was delighted with the treasure, but he was displeased with the message from the Emperor. Montezuma sent word that he was very happy to have the Spaniards visit his country, but it was impossible to see them. The strangers should go home now, knowing that he was their friend.

With proof of the country's wealth before his eyes, the Spanish commander now determined to go to Mexico city with or without the Emperor's invitation. The gifts of Montezuma had aroused in Cortés a burning desire for conquest. If Montezuma could present such fine gifts as these, he thought, what great treasures this country must hold!

Knowing that his men would be hesitant to take part in such a dangerous mission, Cortés destroyed all of his ships but one. There was an angry outcry from the soldiers when they saw their only means of escape cut off. Cunningly, Cortés pointed out the great riches of the land, and said that any cowards could sail back to Cuba in the last remaining vessel. Ashamed of themselves, the soldiers cried, "On to Mexico! On to Mexico!"

Secretly Cortés himself had doubts concerning the march on Mexico city. Although he had some cavalry troops, a few cannon and much better small arms than the Aztecs, still the Indians had thousands of warriors in their ranks. What could four hundred Spaniards do against the Aztec Empire?

Oddly enough, it was the Indian people themselves who strengthened the little army. After a few bloody skirmishes with natives along the coast, Cortés won the respect of the Tlascalan people, a group of Aztecs who were tired of paying heavy taxes and were annoyed by the Emperor's arrogance. With these discontented people Cortés made an alliance, and as a result, he led an army of seven thousand men toward the Aztec capital of Mexico city. When Montezuma heard of the approaching force, he sent messengers with a hasty invitation for Cortés to visit the city. The great Aztec Emperor had an uneasy feeling that his empire was crumbling away. His uneasiness was increased by thoughts of an old Aztec legend which foretold the return of an ancient god. Could Cortés be a god come back to the land of the Aztecs?

For three months the Spaniards and their Indian allies

marched across the hot coastal country, over cool rugged mountains, and on to a broad valley marked by lovely lakes reflecting the blue of the sky. On the waters rode the famous Floating Gardens bright with flowers and plants. Narrow canoes darted here and there along the shores. There lay the beautiful city of Mexico, its towers and temples white in the warm sunshine. Surrounded by water and cut by numerous canals, it stood like a charming Venice of the New World.

Across the waters on a broad stone causeway five miles in length they marched to a bridge that led into the city. Once inside the walls, they were met by the glittering procession of the Emperor. Dressed in a magnificent costume of the finest

cotton sparkling with precious stones, Montezuma rode in a
gold-burnished litter carried on the shoulders of Aztec nobles.
He stepped down to meet the Spaniards, and his striking
appearance impressed even the worldly Cortés. From the tall
green plumes of his headdress to the golden soles of his
sandals, Montezuma looked the mighty Emperor.

Great masses of the Aztec people crowded the streets to
catch first glimpses of the Spaniards in their shining helmets
and breastplates. The prancing horses were animals of
wonder, for they had never before been seen in Mexico. As
Cortés rode through the streets, he passed elaborate flat-roofed
homes smothered in flowers, the little mud huts of the common
people, the wide colourful market places and the massive
temples where captives were sacrified on jasper altars.

III

The Spaniards were made comfortable in one of the royal
palaces. Without relaxing his discipline, Cortés set up sentries
and took all the usual precautions of a military commander.
As the days passed, the Aztecs remained friendly and polite,
but the Spaniards had a strange feeling that Montezuma and
his warriors might turn on them. Cortés realized that his small
force was in a dangerous position surrounded as it was by
hosts of Aztecs. He realized too that if he was to gain control
of the city it must be by swift and ruthless action. Neither
the Emperor nor his people must stand in the way of his
rising ambition. Cortés was not a man who would let his
conscience stand between himself and his desire.

Disregarding the kindness which had been shown by the
Aztecs, Cortés calmly forged a treacherous plan to gain control
of Mexico. Montezuma was seized suddenly and taken to the
quarters of the Spaniards. The unfortunate Emperor, taken

by surprise, was dismayed by his loss of power and freedom, but he felt that there was nothing he could do.

With Montezuma in his power, Cortés was then in a powerful position. Had the Emperor been a strong and courageous leader, he would have commanded his warriors to wipe out the Spaniards by an overwhelming attack, but this he refused to do. A further proof of his weakness lay in the fact that he urged his people to co-operate with the Spaniards. All of this, of course, made it much simpler for Cortés to proceed with his determined plan of conquest.

Cortés took little pity on the captive Emperor, forcing him and his chiefs to recognize the King of Spain as their true Monarch. In so doing he encouraged the belief that he, Cortés, was a god who had come back to the land of the Aztecs. Taking swift advantage of the situation, Cortés demanded that all the cities and provinces of Mexico should give presents to their new king in Spain. So the tax collectors were sent throughout the country and in a short time they returned with huge loads of treasures. This great store of wealth, when finally valued, proved to be worth more than six million dollars in terms of our money. With gloating eyes the Spaniards examined the treasure, each estimating the value of his own share.

Just at the time when Spanish power in Mexico seemed secure, Cortés was faced with serious trouble. His efforts to spread Christianity among the Aztecs met with stubborn resistance from the priests. Even Montezuma protested. Then came the shattering news that an expedition from the Spanish colonies had arrived on the coast. The newcomers had been sent to arrest Cortés for his disobedience to the Governor of Cuba. Without hesitation Cortés marched to the coast with a small band of his soldiers, surprised his countrymen in a night attack and defeated them. He imprisoned the Spanish commander and persuaded the soldiers to join his cause. This victory was scarcely complete when a messenger arrived with a note stating that the Aztecs had rebelled and attacked the Spanish soldiers who had been left in Mexico city. Once again Cortés was on the march, this time accompanied by his new followers.

Shortly after they arrived in the capital city, the palace of the Spaniards was attacked by thousands of Aztec warriors. The attackers tried to climb the walls and set fire to the buildings. Fighting madly, the Spaniards were hard pressed to drive them off. In order to prevent a disaster Cortés forced poor Montezuma to appear on the castle walls and speak to his people. The unfortunate Emperor told his warriors that the Spaniards were his friends and that he was not their prisoner. He asked the Aztecs to stop fighting and go home. If they did this, he said, the Spaniards would leave the city.

Shouting in fury some of the warriors hurled stones and javelins at the Emperor. A large smooth stone struck Montezuma in the head and he dropped senseless to the wall. A strange hush fell over the scene, and then the Aztecs, shocked by the loss of their ruler, fled panic stricken from the scene.

Later Montezuma revived, but the blow received from his own people had broken his heart. Completely humbled in spirit, he cared to live no longer.

Fighting between the Spaniards and the Aztecs went on with renewed fury. The Indians launched attack after attack, bridges were torn down to hinder escape from the city, food supplies dwindled. Then to climax these events . . . Montezuma died. Even Cortés was touched by the passing of the once mighty Emperor, now destroyed by Spanish greed.

IV

The death of Montezuma placed the Spaniards in a most hazardous position.

In Mexico City, Cortés and his men fought battles against the Aztec warriors. See the big pyramidal temples of the Aztecs in the background. In what ways were these different from the pyramids of the Egyptians?

"Those Aztec warriors will stop at nothing now," said Cortés. "We must leave the city!"

In the darkness the Spanish soldiers and the Tlascalans began the long march through the city streets, and alarm spread through the city like the swift approach of a summer storm. Mobs of people gathered to harass the escaping enemy. Showers of stones and arrows rained on the Spaniards and their Indian allies. They fought only to protect themselves, pushing forward doggedly through the darkness. All night long the furious battle raged through the streets, along the causeway and about the broken bridges. Spaniards were killed by flying stones; they slipped from the roadway into the waters; they were captured by the howling Aztecs. Many a Spaniard drowned while still clutching a precious gold object in his stiff fingers. In the morning a tired, battered, discouraged column staggered away from the city. Cortés watched his troops with tears in his eyes.

Finally they reached the coast and rested after the hardships of the march. It was not long, however, before the tireless Cortés was preparing for a return march on the capital. He was fortunate enough to receive more men, arms and ships which arrived from Cuba. These, of course, had not been intended for Cortés, but the determined leader simply seized the ships and encouraged the men to join his army. Some of his old soldiers, tired of life in Mexico, returned to the colonies, but many still remained to take part in the new adventure. So with a larger army of Spaniards and a strong force of Tlascalan warriors he began his third march on Mexico city. Perhaps the strangest equipment carried by the expedition was the material for thirteen ships to be used in the attack on the city. It was unbelievable—thirteen vessels moved over the mountains on the shoulders of men!

On reaching the valley of Mexico, Cortés had his ships assembled and placed in the water. He divided his soldiers and Indians so as to encircle the city, and then began a series of quick attacks by land and water. The ships smashed up masses of Aztec canoes, while raiding parties darted in and out of the city. More and more bands of dissatisfied Indians joined Cortés until he had a vast army under his control. There was suffering on both sides, but the position of the defenders was most difficult. The Aztecs within the walls received very little food from outside, their main water supply was cut off, hundreds died from hunger and disease. Buildings were smashed by cannon fire and dozens more went up in flames. Bodies lay in the streets. The long dreary siege finally came to an end with two vicious battles in which thousands lost their lives. Spanish weapons took a frightful toll, and by August, 1521, the Aztecs were beaten and offered a pitiful surrender.

Hernando Cortés had reached his goal. Mexico was captured and the riches of the Aztec Empire lay at his feet. But at what cost the victory had been won! One of the greatest civilizations of the New World had been ravaged by conquerors and destroyers. Even in an age of violence, it stood out as a savage and ruthless campaign.

The news of Cortés' victory spread to the colonies and across the ocean to Spain. Such bold and successful military action was not to go unrewarded in the Spanish court. Since the King had received a generous share of the Mexican treasure, he forgave Cortés for his disobedience and heaped honours upon him. The conqueror of Mexico was named Governor, Captain-General and Chief Justice of Mexico, or *New Spain* as it came to be called.

The days of glory, however, were not to last. When Cortés died in Spain, 1547, he was poor, lonely and almost forgotten. It is possible that his last days were haunted by unpleasant visions—Aztec gods melted down for gold . . . streets filled with dead and dying . . . blood running over cobble stones . . . the wistful face of the dying Montezuma!

4 THE INCAS

Between five and six thousand years ago a remarkable Indian civilization was born in the heart of the Andes Mountains of South America. Little villages appeared in the dense forests or on the high misty plateaus, and a few of these grew slowly into cities. Powerful leaders joined some of the settlements together and set up little mountain kingdoms. As the centuries rolled by, there gradually developed a great Indian Empire that spread across vast areas of the southern continent.

An old legend tells of the strange beginning of the Inca people. It is the story of a poor family living in a small community near the misty, cold city of Cuzco. Four brothers and four sisters, becoming weary of their toilsome life on the farm, decided that they would seek a more pleasant existence. Trading their wool and their potatoes on the market in Cuzco, they secured quantities of gold thread, coloured wool and small bangles. These purchases continued for many weeks, until they had collected enough material to make two gorgeous golden suits.

Early one morning, before daylight, the family stole into the city and hid in an empty building. Then as the sun came up over the mountains, two members of the family walked into the market-place, dressed in the golden costumes. There they moved in the crowded plaza where Indians shivered about open fires and llamas stood patiently with their loads of salt, wool and potatoes. Then the man and woman in the brilliant garments raised their hands and shouted, "We are Incas— Children of the Sun. We have been sent by the great Sun-god to rule over you."

Strange as it may seem, the people of Cuzco accepted the Children of the Sun as their rulers and their gods. More and more of the natives joined their ranks until the crafty Indians had a powerful following. They ordered the people to construct a large Temple of the Sun in Cuzco and then commenced to broaden their rule over neighbouring tribes. Eventually the original Children of the Sun died, but their children and grandchildren succeeded to power and each ruler expanded his control until a great empire spread for two thousand miles along the coast of South America. It actually included the present countries of Ecuador, Peru, Bolivia, much of Chile, part of northwestern Argentina and some of western Brazil. It is believed that fifteen to twenty-five million people lived in the Empire of the Incas.

Like the Aztecs of Mexico, the Incas reached the height of their power by the year 1500. The capital of the Empire became the city of Cuzco, Peru, which is the oldest permanent city of the Americas, resting high in the clouds eleven thousand feet above sea level. It was a large city filled with many massive buildings made from cut stone. So well constructed were these buildings that numbers of them still remain in good condition. When the Spaniards saw the Temple of the Sun, they said that it was equal to any building in all Europe. An old fortress on the outskirts of the city contained single blocks of stone which measured thirty-eight feet, by eighteen feet, by six feet, and these stone sections had been moved some miles

The Incas worshipped the sun. Here an Inca priest is performing a ceremony in honour of the Sun-God. Notice the huge blocks of stone which were used to make the Inca temple.

from the quarries. Even the builders of the Egyptian pyramids had done no better!

The government of the Incas was a dictatorship, though not excessively cruel. The Inca ruler and his officials completely controlled the lives of the people, managing such affairs as marriage, occupations, land, education, holidays and celebrations. Ten families with a leader in charge formed the smallest group within the state. Ten of these groups formed the next highest unit, ten of these formed the next, and so on up to the ruler himself.

The ruler, or Inca, received the highest respect, for he was not only an earthly monarch but a relative of the Sun-god. No one thought of questioning his authority, and even the highest officials were most humble in his presence. All land in the Empire belonged to the Inca, but it was divided each year for three different purposes. In each community one third of the land was set aside for the government, one third for the gods, and one third for the people. Common people were required to work all lands in turn according to rules set out by the officials of the Inca.

Many craftsmen were employed in the making of clothing, weapons, pottery, tools and ornaments. The work of the craftsmen was set by officials, and boys usually followed the same occupation as their fathers. Each community had its own particular craft, so that some villages specialized in spinning and weaving, some in pottery, some in carving and so on. All articles were collected and distributed according to need. Each family received its share of food and clothing, while the remainder was divided between temples and government. Great storehouses spread across the Empire were stocked with clothing, weapons, food supplies and other equipment. Such stores were often used by the Inca armies.

Once a year a wedding festival was held. If the young people of marriageable age were not already paired off, this was done by a visiting official. Then the mass wedding ceremony took place and proper celebrations were held. Under this system it is not surprising that there were few bachelors and spinsters in the Inca Empire.

The Incas did not provide education as we know it today. The crafts were passed down from father to son and from mother to daughter. There was some simple instruction in agriculture regarding tilling, planting and care of the domestic animals—llama and alpaca. Young members of the nobility were prepared for important offices by schooling under the priests. No written language existed in the land of the Incas, but records and messages could be prepared by a peculiar method of tying knots in pieces of string. The pattern of the knots and the colours of the strings combined to express ideas. This was known as *quipu*.

The common people of the Inca Empire enjoyed the security of a well controlled state. They never went hungry; in old age they were cared for; they were not troubled by robbers and murderers; land and homes were provided for them. However, they did lead a very narrow life—forced to live and work as their rulers commanded, married when ordered to do so, tied fast to their own little communities. There was no chance to rise in life, no chance to accomplish great things. The Incas became a nation of followers, having no will of their own, and this is undoubtedly the reason why they fell such easy victims to the power of the invaders.

5   PIZARRO IN PERU

In 1513, a Spanish adventurer, Nunez de Balboa, crossed the Isthmus of Panama and reached the Pacific. Carrying the Royal Standard of Spain, he waded into the water and claimed the ocean in the name of the Spanish King. With Balboa was a young Spaniard who was to see a great deal more of the Pacific and was to make long voyages along its shores.

I

Francisco Pizarro was a handsome bearded man, strong and courageous—determined as a bulldog. Like Cortés, he went to the Spanish colonies to seek his fortune, and there he found plenty of excitement and adventure. In Panama he made a name for himself as a successful pianter and as a daring soldier. Among his adventures there was the journey with Balboa to the Pacific Ocean, and this thrilling experience only served to increase his desire to travel and explore.

Stories of great treasure in the Inca lands of Peru reached Pizarro, and he decided to make a voyage southward along the coast from Panama. It was possible, he thought, that the unknown lands might prove to be as wealthy as the great Aztec Empire which Cortés had conquered.

Pizarro realized that he could not attempt this adventure alone, so he formed a partnership with a plantation owner, Diego de Almagro, and a priest, Hernando de Luque. The three managed to secure enough money for the first expedition, and in 1524, Pizarro set out with a hundred men and a number of Indian slaves. During the next four years he explored the northwestern coast of South America, enduring hunger, fever, storms and fierce Indians. Several times the partners found themselves bankrupt, but they always managed to secure more ships and more men. Doubtless the whole affair would have been given up had it not been for the determination of Pizarro. He maintained his faith in the wealth of Peru, and held this up as a shining goal to his men.

The first success came when Pizarro reached the coast of Ecuador. Here the Spaniards saw for the first time the civilization of the Incas: their gold, their stone buildings and their system of government. Pizarro was so delighted with discovery that he returned to Panama to report his progress, and then went on to Spain to speak with King Charles V. The Spanish monarch was so greatly impressed by the good news that he named Francisco Pizarro governor of all lands that he might discover.

On his return to the New World Pizarro led an expedition of two hundred and eighty men and one hundred horses southward along the coast of South America. After a number of disappointments his ships landed on the coast of northern Peru. Here the Spaniards learned that the Emperor of the Incas, Atahualpa, was visiting in Cajamarca two hundred miles inland from the coast. It was a long and tiresome journey over high mountain peaks to the city, but Pizarro collected his men and set off on the march. Ten thousand feet they climbed into the cold mist of the passes and plateaus, and then down again on the other side of the range. Pizarro sent a messenger ahead to announce his coming and it was not long before Incas arrived with presents of llamas and a message from the Inca Emperor. Atahualpa had sent a cordial invitation for the Spaniards to visit him.

As Pizarro and his soldiers approached the city of Caja-marca they were alarmed to see a huge encampment of Inca warriors that spread across the mountain slopes. So great was the army that the visitors could not estimate its numbers. This was not a reassuring sight to the little group of Spaniards who hoped to become the conquerors of Peru.

The city itself was deserted when the Spaniards rode into the silent streets. Quickly they established themselves in a number of buildings and made preparations to defend them-selves. Pizarro sent one of his officers, Hernando de Soto, with fifteen horsemen to speak with the Inca monarch, and then waited to see what would happen. De Soto returned to report that Atahualpa would call upon the Spaniards the following day.

Pizarro then was forced into a desperate decision. Should he receive the Inca leader peacefully and run the risk of sudden attack, or should he strike a mighty blow at the Indian army?

The next afternoon the Spaniard watched as the Incas approached the city. It was a glittering procession that moved across the valley. In front of the long line came groups of servants sweeping the Inca's pathway, musicians playing on strange instruments, and members of noble families dressed in colourful garments. Atahualpa himself rode in a golden throne borne on the shoulders of panting Indians.

In the city square Pizarro waited tensely with twenty soldiers at his side. The others of his army were hidden in buildings along the side of the plaza. A Spanish friar advanced calmly to meet the Inca Emperor. There he stood before the haughty ruler, preaching a sermon on Christianity and demanding that the Inca people recognize the King of Spain

as their real ruler. In closing his speech, the friar placed a
Bible in the hands of Atahualpa. The Inca Emperor, annoyed
by the friar's demands, threw the Bible to the ground, saying
that he would recognize no king and that his god was the
Sun-god.

Then followed a savage massacre on the square of Caja-
marca. Pizarro gave the signal for attack: a cannon boomed,
footsoldiers and cavalrymen thundered from the big doorways
of the nearby buildings. In a matter of seconds the plaza was
a surging mass of slashing Spaniards and panic-stricken Incas.
The helpless Indians fell in heaps before the swinging sword
blades and the sharp fire of muskets. Screaming and running
they slipped in pools of blood and fell beneath the hoofs of
the horses. Those who were brave enough to shield Atahualpa
were quickly brushed aside and slaughtered to the last man.
The Inca Emperor was seized and held by the Spanish
troopers. The merciless killing of the Incas went on and on,
across the square and outside the city. Shocked by the
massacre of their comrades and terrified by the swift movements of the galloping horses, the Indian warriors ran for the
mountains. It is not known how many of the Incas lost their
lives, since records give different numbers ranging from two
thousand to ten thousand. Whatever the losses may have
been, one fact remained clear. Pizarro's pitiless action had
smashed an Inca army and had placed the Emperor in his
power. This treacherous victory had been won without the
loss of a single Spanish warrior, and Pizzaro himself was the
only one wounded. He had received an arm wound while
protecting Atahualpa from attack.

II

Although the Emperor of the Incas was a prisoner he was
treated with outward respect by the Spaniards. His own

servants waited on him and he led the life of ceremony to which he was accustomed. Atahualpa was quick to see that the invaders of his country prized gold above all else. This gave him the idea that he might be able to buy his own freedom if he offered enough treasure to Pizarro. He suggested to the Spanish leader that in exchange for liberty he would give all the gold that could be stored in a room to the height of his up-stretched hand. This was no small ransom for the room was seventeen feet wide and twenty-two feet long!

As might be expected, Pizarro agreed willingly to this plan. He had nothing to lose and much to gain by such an agreement. A great treasure would be collected with no effort on the part of the Spaniards. As the weeks went by, loads of gold and silver dishes and ornaments arrived and were placed in the room. The gloating Spaniards watched as the pile grew higher and higher. At last Pizarro agreed that the ransom was paid. Then began the work of dividing the treasure. The results of the magnificent craftsmanship of the Inca goldsmiths was melted down and formed into rough bars of gold that could be easily carried away. The total value of the ransom amounted to more than fifteen million dollars!

When the Inca ransom was securely in his hands, Pizarro faithlessly threw aside his bargain and refused to set free the Emperor. He was afraid to release the Inca, because he might collect armies and overwhelm the Spaniards. Pizarro calmly decided to get rid of Atahualpa and so he invented some ridiculous charges against the Inca ruler. During the course of a single day Pizarro brought Atahualpa to trial, sentenced him to death and carried out the execution. Just before his death, the Inca begged that his body might be sent to Quito. Heartlessly Pizarro ordered that the Emperor be strangled and his body buried at Cajamarca.

Shortly before this time Pizarro's partner, Almagro, had arrived in Peru with one hundred and fifty men to strengthen the forces of the Spaniards. Together the two adventurers marched their troops to Cuzco, capital city of the Incas. The Spanish soldiers ransacked the palaces, the public buildings and the great temple of the Sun. They went mad with joy as they discovered life-sized images, dishes, kettles, bowls, ornaments and even bathtubs made from solid gold. Even more astounding were the gold bars twenty feet in length. This second great treasure secured in Peru by the Spaniards was worth more than seven million dollars.

Pizarro's men tramped through the Empire looting and destroying as they went. They helped themselves to the goods in the Inca storehouses and slaughtered herds of llamas for food.

When Pizarro became Governor of Peru, it was decided

Pizarro was killed by a small group of Spanish rebels one evening while he was having dinner. Here in this picture the conqueror of Peru lies dying on the floor.

that the Incas should be given a puppet ruler from their own royal family. Accordingly a nephew of Atahualpa, named Manco Capac, was crowned as Emperor. This boy appeared to be weak and harmless, but later he proved that he had a mind of his own.

Pizarro and his partner, jealous of each other, quarrelled between themselves, and Almagro went off to conquer Chile.

The young Inca Emperor, Manco Capac, was set free by Pizarro on the promise that he would secure a large golden image for the Spaniards. As soon as the lad was free he rallied a large army of Inca warriors and attacked the city of Cuzco. The Spaniards, surrounded by thousands of enemy troops, fought on in the blazing city. The siege continued until the Spaniards grew weak from hunger and fatigue. Finally the Incas withdrew from the mountains, but they continued to bother the Spaniards by swift fierce raids.

It was not the Incas, however, who caused the violent deaths of the two Spanish partners. Destruction came through their own bitter jealousy. Almagro returned from an unsuccessful expedition to Chile and imprisoned several relatives of Pizarro's. In revenge the Spanish commander seized Almagro and put him to death. A party of rebels led by Almagro's son surprised Pizarro one day while he was dining. A quick sword thrust caught Pizarro in the throat and he fell gasping to the floor. Dipping a finger in his own blood, he marked a cross on the floor, and died whispering the word, "Jesu."

Although the conqueror of Peru was gone, the Spaniards continued to hold the land of the Incas, and wealth moved from South America to the coffers of Spain. Never again did the Inca people recover the glory of former days. Their treasures, their storehouses and their system of government were gone forever.

6   HERNANDO DE SOTO

Among the men whom Pizarro had taken to Peru was a dashing young officer, Hernando de Soto, who unlike his commander came out of the campaign alive. The Peruvian adventure had been a very profitable one for de Soto, as he came away with a personal fortune worth at least half a million dollars. Then, as a wealthy man, he had married a Spanish lady and lived in a magnificent castle.

Seamen moved about the docks, officers bellowed commands, grunting Indians carried heavy bundles on their bent backs to the open hatches that yawned in the decks of Spanish vessels.

"Come on! Faster! Faster!" cried the Spaniards as they prodded the frightened slaves.

Into the holds of the vessels went a bewildering assortment of materials and equipment: food supplies, lumber, nails, tools, leather, gunpowder, bullets, cannon balls, crossbows, arrows, armour, seeds and grain. Hernando de Soto watched his ships from the docks and his dark eyes sparkled with anticipation.

"When shall we be ready to leave?" he asked one of his officers.

"Two days, sir!"

"Good!" said de Soto. "Hoist anchor as soon as possible."

He smiled to himself as he continued to watch the busy, noisy activity of the Cuban port. "I'm a very fortunate man," he thought. "Here I am almost ready for a voyage to Florida, and with the King's permission signed and sealed. Who knows what treasures lie to the north? It could be that there is another Mexico or another Cuzco along the coast or deep in the forests!"

On a May day in 1539, two hundred and fifty horses, three

In Cuba, Indian slaves loaded De Soto's sailing ships in preparation for a voyage to Florida. The ships carried food, weapons, armour, seeds, lumber, horses and pigs.

hundred pigs and six hundred and fifty men were placed aboard the little fleet and chains rattled as the anchors were hoisted. De Soto sailed northward from Cuba into the Gulf of Mexico and six days later he was off the coast of west Florida near Tampa Bay.

As the ships neared shore, the Timucan Indians sent up dark smoke signals against the blue sky, and this warning of danger passed from village to village, northward and southward through the Indian country. De Soto landed on an island and occupied a deserted settlement, Ucita, which had been an Indian capital town. De Soto and his officers took over the chief's house as a dwelling, while a Timucan temple was torn down and its timbers used to construct barracks for the troops. Frightened by the strength of the invaders, the Indians kept away from the settlement, contenting themselves with guerrilla attacks on roaming Spanish scouts. The chief of the Timucans proved to be hostile to the Spaniards, but a lesser chief was friendly and this division of the Indian people probably saved the Spaniards from full scale attack.

One day a party of forty horsemen met a small group of Timucans and were on the point of cutting them down with swords, when a tattered figure stepped from among the Indians and shouted, "Seville . . . Seville . . . Christian . . . Christian!" To the astonishment of the Spaniards they discovered that the tanned figure in native clothing was a Spanish man, Juan Ortiz, who had been captured years before by the Timucans. The poor fellow in the excitement of the moment could only remember two words from his own language. Ortiz remained with de Soto, and proved to be very useful, as he spoke the Indian tongue.

Most of the vessels in the fleet returned to Cuba, but a few were kept in Florida for exploration and communication with the colonies. During July de Soto sent off one of these vessels with a report to the Spanish government on the progress of

DE SOTO EXPLORATIONS

the expedition. Dissatisfied with the wealth to be found in the region of Tampa Bay, de Soto took his men, horses, pigs, and moved off in a northerly direction. The Indians he met continued to speak of great treasure to be found further north, and de Soto kept his column marching through the forests beyond Florida and into the lands which we now call the Southern States. In many places the Indians proved to be a nuisance, ambushing the Spaniards as they pushed forward. The raiding Indians grew particularly fond of pork and delighted in attacking the pens where the pigs were kept at night. De Soto frequently presented friendly chiefs with a pair of pigs as a generous present. It has been said that the razor-back hogs which still live in southern regions of the United States are descendants of de Soto's pigs, but we are not sure that this is so.

After leaving Florida, de Soto moved in a general north-westerly direction through Georgia, Carolina and Tennessee. It was a rugged, desperate march for the Spaniards. Horses died, shoes and clothing wore out, men were killed by Indian arrows and disease and fatigue sapped their strength. Added to these difficulties was the warm, humid climate. The cities of gold were never found, but de Soto went on doggedly, always hoping that his goal lay just ahead, across the forest or swamp.

After three years of this gruelling travel they reached the Mississippi River near the spot where the city of Memphis now stands. Even the discovery of the great waterway did not cheer the disappointed leader. He was interested in treasure. A new river meant nothing. At one time de Soto's camp lay but a few miles away from that of another Spanish explorer, Francisco de Coronado, but the two men never met.

During the summer of 1542, de Soto, then tired and dis-couraged, developed a fever and died. In order to keep his death a secret from the Indians, his men dropped his body at night into the river near the west bank. Another Spanish explorer had lost his life in the long quest for the golden cities.

At the time of de Soto's death only half of the members of his expedition were still alive, and these hastily decided to make their way back to the colonies as well as they could. They built a number of boats, made their way down the Mississippi and eventually reached Spanish territory in northern Mexico.

7   JACQUES CARTIER

To the French the successes of the Spanish in the New World were both astounding and alarming. It is true that Breton French fishermen had become familiar with the fishing grounds off the east coast of America, but it is equally true that France had neither founded colonies nor explored new lands. King Francis I decided that it was time to take action if France was to share in the spoils of the Americas. To command an expedition, he chose a well known master pilot of St. Malo, a man who had many years experience at sea. At one time, he may have been a pirate, and it is even possible that he had once sailed on a voyage to Brazil.

I

On a warm spring day, April 1534, the little harbour of St. Malo, France, was alive with colour and movement. White gulls wheeled above two tall sailing ships that rode quietly beside the ancient wharves. Groups of sober citizens watched tensely as soldiers and sailors marched aboard and made the last quick preparation for departure. Officers shouted commands, sailors ran up the rigging—the townsmen drew in closer. On shore little girls stared anxiously, their mothers wiped tears from smarting eyes, and old men looked wistfully at the stirring vessels.

On the bridge of his ship, Jacques Cartier ran a broad hand through his dark beard and spoke crisply to one of his officers. "Hoist anchor," he ordered. "Now is the time to leave."

Up came the anchors and the ships drifted slowly away, leaving a broad ripple in the calm water of the harbour.

"Bon voyage, bon voyage, Jacques Cartier!" called the townsmen.

Cartier and his men cast a last fond look over the old seaport and then turned to the open sea.

The ships pushed across the Atlantic, rounded the top of Newfoundland and sailed southward through the Strait of Belle Isle. The whole length of this route was known to the French through the voyages of fishermen, but soon they came to unknown waters. Along bleak shores Cartier's ships made their way to the open spaces of the Gulf of St. Lawrence. After the lonely northern coast the green islands of the gulf seemed strangely lush and fertile.

By July 2, the ships had crossed the gulf and could go no farther. Turning northward, they skirted the shores of what is now New Brunswick and finally came to a deep bay. The weather turned exceedingly warm and the seamen sweltered on the decks. The high temperatures made such an impression on Cartier that he named the place Chaleur Bay (Bay of Heat).

In this general region the French met numbers of Huron and Algonquin Indians who had come to the coast to do their summer fishing. These tribesmen were very friendly and showed a keen interest in trading. They were willing to give up anything they owned in exchange for metal articles such as knives, hatchets, kettles and ornaments. Cartier became acquainted with their chief and persuaded him to let his two sons return to France in order to learn the French language. They would be back, Cartier promised, the following year.

On the coast of Gaspé the seamen erected a massive

wooden cross and Cartier claimed the land in the name of France. Sailing northward, they reached the low coastline of Anticosti Island. There in the mouth of the mighty St. Lawrence, they saw open water spreading away to the west and felt the tug of the river current on their rudders.

Three months after leaving France, Cartier ordered his ships back to St. Malo, so they left the gulf by way of the Strait of Belle Isle and headed eastward across the swell of the Atlantic. In the King's court Cartier reported that he had found fertile islands, tall trees, good fisheries and bountiful game—but there were no cities, no emperors and no shining palaces. The people living in the new lands, he said, were poor Indians who owned nothing of value.

King Francis was disappointed, but he still held hope for better things in America. After all, Cartier had sighted open water to the west of Anticosti Island. Perhaps this was a passage to the Orient. Then too, the Indian boys who came to France with Cartier, spoke of three Indian kingdoms along the St. Lawrence. Perhaps these kingdoms held magnificent cities like those the Spanish had found to the south. King Francis pondered the question and then ordered Cartier back to the New World the following year.

II

In May, 1535, Cartier was once again on the Atlantic, his ships' bows pointed toward the Gulf of St. Lawrence. After some careful exploration of the gulf coast, he asked the two Indian lads to guide the vessels up the great river. During the mellow days of late summer they moved up the wide waterway, enjoying the colourful scenery. It was a glorious experience for the sailors. Little islands glowed with hanging grapes, fruits and nuts. Schools of fish wriggled and shone in the clear waters. Whales, seals and walruses played and lolled.

Pudgy sea-cows rose to the surface with their young hugged tightly beneath broad flippers. Song birds gave concerts from the shores and seabirds screamed aloft.

Below the dark cliffs where the city of Quebec now stands, the vessels came to anchor. Chief Donnacona and his tribesmen from the nearby village of Stadacona came to welcome the palefaced men in the big ships. Through his two Indian boys, Cartier was able to talk with the friendly villagers. He said that he wished to remain at Stadacona for the winter, but before doing so he planned to travel farther up the river.

Chief Donnacona was pleased to have the French stay at his village, but he was not at all anxious to have his guests go further. He did not care to share his trading privileges with the other Indians. Donnacona and the two Indian lads did everything possible to persuade Cartier to remain at Stadacona. They described the dangers of the trip, the swirling rapids,

At Stadacona, Indians, dressed in dog skins and long horns, tried to keep Cartier from visiting the Indian village of Hochelaga. Do you think these **warriors frightened the French?**

the hostile Indians and the cold weather. When these arguments failed, three Indians were dressed as devils. The warriors, in dog skins, long horns and blackened faces, pranced about and warned Cartier that if he went to Hochelaga, he would die. The Frenchman smiled.

Late in September Cartier and some of his men took one of the smaller vessels with two row boats and started the voyage up river. In twelve days they came to the large village of Hochelaga on the spot where the city of Montreal now stands. This was a well fortified settlement surrounded by three wooden stockades which encircled fifty huge lodges. Beyond the walls were the well-tilled fields of grains and vegetables. The villagers were delighted at the arrival of the visitors, and all clamoured to take part in the welcome. To the Indians, Cartier was almost a god. So great was their belief in him that they brought their sick and wounded for healing. Cartier, moved by their faith in his power, put his hands on the suffering natives and read passages from the Gospel of St. John. It is a strange fact that a similar scene took place that same year away to the southwest of the St. Lawrence, when a Spanish explorer, Cabeza de Vaca, visited tribes of southern Indians.

Cartier climbed a high hill overlooking the village and thrilled to the scene that lay below him. To the north he could see the purple outline of the Laurentian mountains, to the southwest the seething Lachine Rapids on the St. Lawrence River, and all around the forests aflame with autumn colour. It was a view to excite the heart of an explorer, a view to love and remember for a lifetime. To the hill Cartier gave the name "Mont Royal" which was later shortened to Montreal.

Cartier had come over a thousand miles from the Gulf of St. Lawrence and still the river flowed from the westward. There were no signs of a passage to the Orient and certainly no gleaming cities rose from the depths of the forest. Cartier had no way of knowing that this broad land was rich in minerals—asbestos, gold, silver, iron and titanium. He did not know that some day men with airplanes and dynamite, bull-dozers and Geiger counters, would extract fortunes from the rugged hills.

In three weeks' time Cartier was back at Stadacona, to find that the men left behind had built a small fort, set up a few cannon and made other preparations for the winter. Anxious to be on the best possible terms with the Indians, Cartier went about making friends and distributing gifts.

Snow came. The days grew colder and colder. Bitter winds whipped about the fort, whistled through the cracks and chilled the shivering Frenchmen. The horrible disease of scurvy appeared among the Indians and soon spread to the alarmed seamen. They grew pale and weak, suffering from aches and pains in their joints. Teeth loosened and dropped from bleeding gums. One after another they fell to the cruel malady, until at one time there were only ten men able to move about and assist the others. Twenty-five Frenchmen died and were buried in the snow. In terror the survivors appealed to heaven for help, putting up black crosses in the snow and chanting solemn hymns of prayer.

It is possible that the whole expedition might have been wiped out during the winter, had not Cartier discovered an Indian cure for scurvy. After cutting bark from an evergreen tree, he placed this in hot water and gave the brew to his suffering crews. This remedy had quick and miraculous effect upon the health of the seamen. They recovered from the disease and gained normal health once more.

Spring came with the melting snow, the rumble of ice in the river and the honking of wild geese in the clear skies. Those must have been days of pure pleasure to the men who had been imprisoned all winter. During the first week in May they set up a tall wooden cross, claiming the land for King Francis. The puzzled Indians watched the ceremony, little knowing what it meant. If they could have foreseen the future years, they might have been tempted to massacre the Frenchmen in the shadow of their cross.

Just before sailing on the return trip to France, Cartier ordered the capture of Donnacona and several other Indians. These were bundled aboard the ships, and the sails were hoisted on the creaking masts. The chief's people were aroused by this treacherous act, but Cartier calmed them by promises of a quick return.

In France, Cartier displayed the kidnapped Donnacona and his tribesmen in the court of King Francis. It must have been a colourful scene—the dark skinned chief in buckskin and feathers talking to Francis I in his robes of state. In the flowing language of the Indian people, Donnacona described his village and the great rolling country that spread away from the river.

III

The country of France was engaged in a European war at the time, so that it was not easy for the King to arrange another voyage to America. Five years passed away. Then Francis chose a nobleman, Roberval, to become the first Viceroy to the French lands overseas, and he ordered a settlement to be founded on the St. Lawrence. Jacques Cartier was named commander of the ships that were to sail with the expedition. The complete company, according to plan, was to consist of four hundred sailors, three hundred soldiers, a group of craftsmen and a few women. This was no small expedition for that time.

Roberval was slow in making his preparations, so Cartier set off with five ships. After reaching Newfoundland, the fleet waited six weeks for the nobleman, but he did not appear.

Impatient with the delay, Cartier sailed up the St. Lawrence and reached Stadacona late in August. Quite naturally, the Indians there inquired for their chief, Donnacona, and the others who had been taken to France. Cartier replied that Donnacona had died, but the others were living in France as lords. This, of course, was untrue. Records show that the Indians all died in lonely exile from their own land.

The ships were moved up-river a few miles west of Stadacona, and there a fort was built. Two vessels of the fleet were sent back to France to report the events of the expedition. Once again French seamen suffered from cold and scurvy, but they managed to pass away the cold months of the winter season. Excitement gripped the party when the men discovered among the rocks, shiny rocks and bits of stone that glittered and glowed like silver, gold and diamonds. With

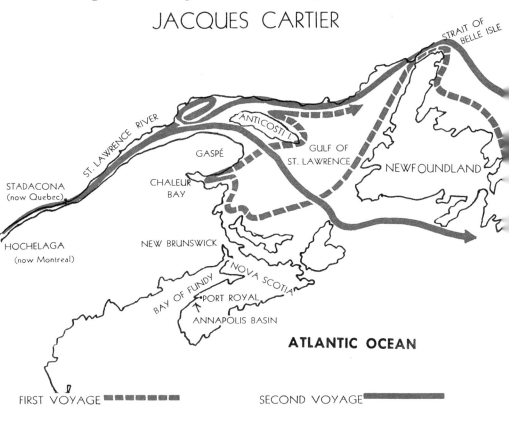

JACQUES CARTIER

shaking fingers they gathered masses of these and stored them in barrels. Their hearts leaped and their eyes shone with feverish joy. Here were great treasures like those of the Aztecs and the Incas! Months later their rising hopes slid down to gloom. Their massive treasures were nothing more than quartz crystals, iron pyrites, mica and corundum—completely worthless in value.

When the river was free of ice in the spring, the vessels pulled away from shore and sailed down the river to the Gulf of St. Lawrence. At Newfoundland Cartier fell in with the fleet of Roberval, and there is reason to believe that the mariner was not pleased with this encounter, since he wanted nothing more than to sail for France. He told Roberval that he was leaving the St. Lawrence because of the hostility of the Indians. This had no effect upon the Viceroy, for he ordered Cartier to accompany his fleet back up the river. Cartier appeared to agree with this arrangement, but during the night his ships disappeared into the blackness, and the next day they were well out on the Atlantic.

Roberval, left alone, made his way up past Stadacona and spent a dreary winter there. It appears that he lost a number of men from scurvy and they all suffered from hunger. Fortunately they had little trouble with the Indians. During the spring months he made some explorations, but the record in this regard is not clear. By the autumn of 1543 he was back in France.

Jacques Cartier remained high in the King's favour, and was granted an estate and manor house in the countryside near St. Malo. It is even possible that he was made a nobleman. He died of the plague in 1557.

During the passage of time his burial place was forgotten, but a few years ago a French-Canadian scholar discovered papers in France which stated that Cartier had been buried in the old cathedral in St. Malo.

8 CHAMPLAIN, THE FATHER OF NEW FRANCE

Following the voyages of Jacques Cartier, French fishermen continued to visit the eastern shores of Canada, but these men took little interest in the land that lay beyond the fisheries. It was more than sixty years after Cartier's last bitter winter on the St. Lawrence that another adventurer made important discoveries for France in the New World.

I

Samuel de Champlain was born in the small seaport of Brouage on the coast of France. His father was a sea captain, so it was natural that the boy should become interested in ships, sails and the sea. It is probable that as a lad he learned much of vessels and navigation, but oddly enough he became a soldier rather than a sailor, and fought for ten years in French civil wars. He appears to have been a fine officer, for he won the praise of the French King.

When he left the French army, his early interest in the sea returned. His greatest desire was to sail a ship across the Atlantic to the New World, and in a short time he did that very thing. Through an uncle, who was in the service of the Spanish King, he secured a commission as captain of a Spanish

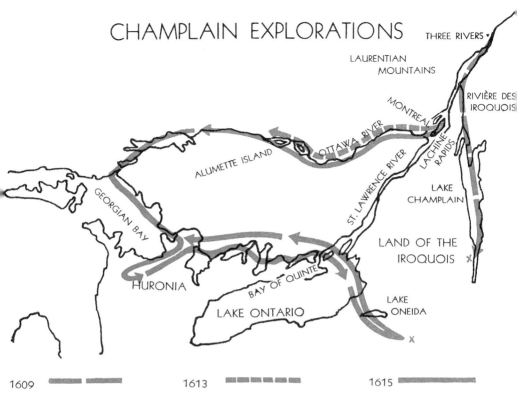

CHAMPLAIN EXPLORATIONS   THREE RIVERS

LAURENTIAN
MOUNTAINS

RIVIÈRE DES
IROQUOIS

MONTREAL

OTTAWA RIVER

ALUMETTE ISLAND

LACHINE RAPIDS

LAKE
CHAMPLAIN

GEORGIAN BAY

ST. LAWRENCE RIVER

LAND OF THE
IROQUOIS   x

HURONIA

BAY OF QUINTE

LAKE ONTARIO

LAKE
ONEIDA

x

1609   1613   1615

vessel sailing to the colonies. This was a thrilling voyage for Champlain, since he visited the West Indies, Panama and Mexico. On his return home, he wrote a book of his adventures. His writing caused such great interest in France that Champlain was named Geographer to the King.

Sailing now under the French flag, he made a voyage to the St. Lawrence River in 1603. This was not an important trip from the standpoint of discovery, but it did show the French people a way of making fortunes in America. There were no great treasures of gold such as Cortés found in Mexico and Pizarro found in Peru, but there was the fur trade. The glossy furs that could be secured from the Indians in exchange for cheap trinkets offered a new and exciting business for French adventurers.

The following year Champlain was back in the New World with an expedition under the command of a French nobleman, de Monts. The purposes of the voyage were to trade in furs,

to Christianize the Indians, and to find a northerly route to the
Orient. Champlain was the geographer of the party. Their
two ships sailed into the Bay of Fundy and the seamen looked
about for a suitable place of location. The first winter was
such a harrowing experience that they moved next spring to
a more pleasant location on Annapolis Basin across the Bay of
Fundy. Here they built a "habitation" and gave it the name
Port Royal.

Today outside the town of Annapolis Royal, Nova Scotia,
you can see the buildings just as they were in the days of
Champlain. These, of course, are not the old buildings of
1605. The present "habitation" was erected a few years ago
from the original plans found in France. There you can see,
built about a small square, the blacksmith shop, the chapel,
the bakery, the kitchen, the dining room, the chambers for
the gentlemen, and upstairs the great dormitory for the
soldiers and workers. It is a quaint and romantic reminder of
the past, standing as it does on the exact spot of the old
"habitation."

During his days at Port Royal, Champlain founded the
Order of Good Cheer. This was a social club for the gentlemen
of the party. Each of the men in turn was required to make
arrangements for the dinner of the day. These were such
happy events that the spirits of the French were kept high.
They dined well and suffered very little from scurvy. It is
interesting to note that the Order has been revived by the
Nova Scotian government, and its grand master is our
Governor-General. You can become a member by spending
at least seven days in Nova Scotia.

II

The French left Port Royal in 1607 when the charter for
the fur trade was taken back by the King. However, the next

year Champlain returned to America, sailing up the St. Lawrence River to the spot where the Indian village of Stadacona had stood. There below the cliffs he landed his men and at once they began the building of a habitation. This was a large two storey building surrounded by a palisade and a moat. Like an old castle it had a large entrance gate and a drawbridge. Long galleries ran around the upper storey. There were storerooms, sleeping quarters for men and officers, a blacksmith shop, a powder magazine and a platform for cannon.

During his first days at Quebec Champlain narrowly missed the fate of Pizarro, for a small group of his men plotted to kill him. They planned to strangle or shoot him during the night. Fortunately the plot was discovered and the leader was executed.

The new arrivals soon became acquainted with the Indians of the St. Lawrence Valley and the Ottawa River. The tribesmen belonging to the Huron and Algonquin tribes brought their furs to Quebec and traded freely with the French. A third tribe, the Iroquois, living to the south of the river did not trade at the habitation, and Champlain learned that they were old enemies of the Hurons and Algonquins. It became clear that the French could not remain on peaceful terms with both of these Indian groups, so Champlain chose to build up a friendship with the Indians that lived nearby. The Algonquins and Hurons became his allies and the Iroquois his enemies.

Champlain carried on the fur trade, but he was even more interested in exploration. The idea of finding a passage through or around America still lay in the back of his mind. One year after the founding of Quebec he joined a war party of tribesmen moving southward into the Iroquois country. In the band there were Champlain, two French soldiers and sixty Indians travelling in twenty-four birchbark canoes. Indian scouts

The wooden shields of the Iroquois were no protection from French gunpowder and shot.

ranged ahead, the main body followed and a few hunters brought up the rear. As they came close to the Iroquois towns, they gathered together into one group and progressed cautiously, lighting no fires and moving by night. Finally they reached a long narrow body of water which we now call Lake Champlain. While following the western shore of the lake they met a group of Iroquois, on July 29, 1609. The time was late in the afternoon.

A battle between the two parties was arranged in a very polite manner. Two canoes of Algonquins visited the Iroquois and enquired if they wished to fight. The Iroquois, of course, replied that they would be delighted, but it was late in the day; they suggested that the battle begin at dawn.

At daybreak the Iroquois warriors advanced calmly toward the crude barricade which had been hastily erected by the Algonquins. Champlain, dressed in light armour and carrying his arquebus, led a group of Indians toward the advancing enemy. As the two parties faced each other, the Iroquois paused in surprise at the appearance of the French leader. Then, as the red men raised their bows, Champlain fired his arquebus with a shocking roar that echoed across the lake. Two of the Iroquois chiefs fell, their wooden armour pierced by the shot. Indian arrows whistled through the trees. A second gun barked from the shelter of the forest and a third Iroquois chief dropped. The mysterious death of their leaders brought sudden fear to the haughty Iroquois. They turned and ran from the scene, pursued by the three Frenchmen and shrieking Algonquins.

Although Champlain had won a battle, he had gained the hatred of the powerful Iroquois people, a hatred that lasted through the years and which at times threatened to wipe out the colonies of France.

Four more years passed before Champlain was able to make another trip into the endless forests that spread away in all directions from Quebec. A young French woodsman, Nicolas Vignau, after a journey up the Ottawa River, told Champlain that he had reached the ocean and that he had seen the wreck of an English ship. Naturally Champlain was interested in the story, for he thought that the northern sea described by Vignau might be a passage to the Orient. He decided to go and see for himself. In May, 1613, he set off from Quebec with four other Frenchmen, one Indian and Vignau. They paddled steadily up the Ottawa, meeting many difficulties with rapids and dense forests along the shores. At one place Champlain almost lost his life in the swift current. Finally they reached Alumette Island and here Champlain was told by the Indians that Vignau had not travelled beyond that point. The young woodsman had invented the story of the northern sea, hoping to get a reward for reporting such an important discovery. Champlain was furious with Vignau's dishonesty, and the Indians would have been very happy to kill him. Discouraged, Champlain returned to Quebec.

During the course of his Ottawa River journey Champlain lost a large, circular, metal instrument called an astrolabe which he used for calculating his position. Strangely enough the instrument was found in 1867, two hundred and fifty-four years after it disappeared.

Two years after this disappointing expedition Champlain began his most important journey of exploration. The Hurons had been begging him for some time to lead another war party into the lands of their enemies. The Iroquois, they said, had become so bold that they were preventing the Hurons and Algonquins from reaching Quebec with their furs. Champlain finally agreed to the plan and left Quebec in 1615, with a band of Hurons. The party paddled up the Ottawa and then crossed to Georgian Bay. They then turned southward along the western shore of Georgian Bay, coming to the lands of the Hurons. Here they were joined by hundreds of warriors, all eager to fight the Iroquois. By a series of lakes and rivers they came to Lake Ontario at the Bay of Quinte. From there they paddled around the eastern end of Lake Ontario and reached the southern shore. After hiding their canoes in the forest, they marched overland toward an Iroquois fort located near Lake Oneida.

The fort, they found, was strongly protected by a palisade thirty feet in height. Champlain ordered the construction of a wooden tower higher than the walls of the fort, since he hoped to place on it the French soldiers, so that they could fire on the Indians inside the stronghold. Wooden shields too were prepared for the Hurons and Algonquins of his party. The plan was to advance behind the shields and set fire to the fort while the French poured volleys of shot from the wooden tower.

When the attack was launched everything went wrong.

The Indians threw away their shields, the fire was badly placed, the flames blew away from the walls, and all turned into confusion. There was so much shouting and running about that Champlain's orders could not be heard. He tried without success to bring order to the attack. The Hurons and Algonquins fell back and refused to rally for further assaults. Then the miserable retreat began. Champlain, suffering from two leg wounds, was treated as any wounded brave. He was tied securely so that he could not move, and then hoisted to the back of a powerful warrior. Actually he suffered more from the roughness of the transportation than he did from the pain in his knee. Afterwards he said that in his whole life he had never suffered such discomfort.

The Hurons and Algonquins withdrew rapidly to Lake Ontario, recovered their canoes, and paddled around the end of the lake. Champlain wished to go directly to Quebec, but the Indians were not willing to spare men and canoes for this purpose. There was no other choice for the French leader; he was forced to accompany the Indians back to the Huron country and to spend the winter there. During the spring of 1616 he had an opportunity to make further explorations in the direction of Lake Superior, but at that time a violent quarrel broke out between the Hurons and the Algonquins. Fearing that this might lead to serious warfare, Champlain remained to settle the dispute. It had been a hard, uncomfortable winter for Champlain living as he did in the dirty, cold huts of the Hurons, but it did give him an opportunity to observe the customs and manners of the Indians. All of his careful observations were later recorded in a book called *The Voyage of 1615.*

III

That was the last important trip of exploration that Champlain ever made. During the next nineteen years of his life he was busy with the duties of governing New France. He faced many difficult problems. The French government thought of the colony as being a mere trading centre. Neither the government nor the fur traders were interested in sending settlers to the new land. This was a great disappointment to Champlain, because he wished to see people clearing land and making farms in the forest. The traders were completely selfish in their treatment of the Indians, and did not hesitate to cheat them. The liquor supplied to the red men caused tragedy and hardship in the Indian villages.

The few buildings that made up Quebec were all built along the water's edge. Louis Hébert was the first settler to clear land and build a home on the heights overlooking the river. Here on ten acres of land he grew vegetables, grains and apples. A few head of cattle were kept in his barn. Indeed, Hébert is often called "The First Candian Farmer."

Récollet friars had come to Canada to do missionary work among the Indians and lived in a convent in Quebec. Later the Jesuits came to New France and these priests are re-membered for their faithful and heroic efforts in the missions of Huronia.

The colony grew so slowly that twenty years after its founding, there were not more than a hundred people in Quebec. This was a far different situation from that of the British settlement in Virginia, where four thousand had settled into solid homes and were growing rich crops of tobacco. It is no wonder that Champlain was discouraged by the slow growth of New France.

Champlain was pleased when a new company was given the right to the fur trade in the valley of the St. Lawrence. The members of the company agreed to bring out three hundred new settlers each year and enough priests to look after the needs of the people. The prospect was more promis-ing than it had been at any previous time. Probably New

France would have progressed rapidly had not France and England become engaged in another war. In 1629 a small fleet of British ships under Captain David Kirke sailed up the St. Lawrence, and Quebec surrendered. Champlain had neither the men nor the arms for a proper defence of the colony. It was a sad time for Champlain. It appeared as if the work of his lifetime had been wasted in useless effort.

When he reached England aboard an English ship, Champlain heard some amazing news—England and France had signed a peace treaty several weeks before the fall of Quebec. This meant, of course, that Kirke had captured the city after fighting between the two countries had stopped. There was good reason to believe that New France would be returned to France, and that is what happened in 1632.

Although Champlain was an old man by this time, he was

Champlain returned to Quebec to rebuild his beloved colony after its capture by the English. Here we see the old explorer waving to the Indians who waited on shore to welcome him.

happy to sail back to Quebec and to take charge once more. In a touching ceremony the friendly Indians welcomed Champlain back to their country, and made long speeches saying how much they had missed him.

The old governor set to work restoring his shattered, burned-out colony, putting up new buildings and strengthening the defences. Slowly the colony began to grow, the Jesuits worked among the Indians, the fur trade expanded, a fort was built at Three Rivers and some land exploration was completed. These were happy years for Champlain; he could see that all his efforts were finally bringing results. He felt confident that New France was now solidly placed in the Valley of the St. Lawrence.

In October, 1635, the old soldier became ill and on Christmas Day he passed peacefully away.

The progress which had begun with Champlain was destined to continue for more than a century. Through settlement, the attempts at farming, the fur trade, the relations with friendly Indians and the work of the missionaries he set a pattern which was to make New France an important colony. Champlain, in fact, laid the cornerstone of Canada.

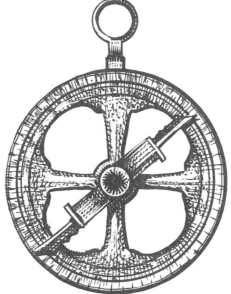

Champlain's astrolabe.

9 JOLIET AND MARQUETTE

As the French colony in the St. Lawrence Valley grew, the fur traders travelled further afield, westward to the Great Lakes and almost to the rim of the prairies. Here they heard tales from the Indians of a mighty river, the "Father of Waters," or the "Missippi" which swept away to the south below the Great Lakes. These stories reached Quebec and caused eager discussions between the Governor, Count Frontenac, and the Intendant, Jean Talon. As a result they planned an expedition to search for the river of the Indian tales. There was always the chance, they thought, that such a waterway might lead to the Pacific. To carry out the work of exploration the Governor chose a tall, rugged woodsman, Louis Joliet, and a delicate Jesuit priest, Father Marquette.

Anxious to be off, Joliet made his way in the late autumn to Mackinac near the present city of Sault Ste. Marie, and there he found Father Marquette at his mission station of St. Ignace.

Winter was too close at hand to start the journey southwards, so the two eager men had to be content to spend the cold months in preparation for the adventure. Carefully they collected from the Indians all the information that they could regarding the land below the lakes. When this was complete, they drew a map to guide them on the first stages of the journey. It was a good map, and surprisingly accurate, as they found later.

Spring came at last. Joliet breathed the fresh warm air and sighed with pleasure. "Look, Father," he shouted, "the water is almost clear of ice. We shall be off in a short time!"

On May 17, 1673, they left St. Ignace with five Indians and a food supply of dried berries, smoked meat and some Indian corn. Father Marquette took a last look at his beloved mission and then stepped into one of the waiting canoes. Paddles dipped, and they were off on the search for the big river.

Skirting the western shore of Lake Michigan, they reached Green Bay, paddled up the Fox River and came to two Indian villages that stood on a height of land dividing the streams that flowed to the Great Lakes from those of the Mississippi Valley. The good-natured villagers helped them move the canoes and packs over the hill and down the other side to the Wisconsin River. It was not a long nor a difficult portage.

For seven days they paddled easily down the Wisconsin, and then the Frenchmen sat up straight and looked ahead. Through the trees they caught sight of broad waters glinting silver in the sunlight. The two canoes broke from the shadow of the forest and glided into the vast stream. Along the shores the water lay smooth as glass, but in the heart of the mighty river the current moved with depth and power. It was the *Missippi*—The Father of Waters!

Joliet's eyes glowed! Father Marquette bowed his head in prayer.

Turning into the flow, they pushed southward. The weather was delightful with clear skies and warm sunshine that slanted over the trees and bounced glitteringly from the ripples on the water. Joliet revelled in the experience as he sang songs and shouted at the water birds. Day after day they floated on. In the evenings they dragged the canoes ashore, lit fires, cooked some food, and then rolled into blankets spread below the starlit skies.

On and on they went . . . in the dark shadow of forests . . . by ghostly swamps . . . along the edges of sweeping prairies dotted with buffalo herds. Giant catfish, dashing about in the shallows, blundered into the canoes, almost swamping the fragile craft.

The Indians that they met during the first part of the travels were friendly and gracious. A group of Illinois tribesmen presented them with a long-stemmed pipe as a peace token, and this later proved a gift of great importance. Joliet used it several times when meeting strange Indians, and found that it worked like magic. All he had to do was wave the pipe over his head, and the strange tribesmen accepted him as a friend. Nevertheless as they moved southward, they took

After walking a few miles from the Mississippi River across the plains, Joliet and Marquette came to an Indian camp where the Indians lived in tepees. The Indians gave signs of peace and friendship.

precautions against surprise attacks, posting sentinels at night, and lighting fires only when necessary.

Late in June they found human footprints along the shore, and after some investigation discovered a well-marked trail leading off to the west. Joliet decided to follow the path in the hope that an Indian village lay nearby. For six miles the party tramped across the grassland and then came in sight of a large encampment. Joliet shouted, then held his breath in suspense. Dogs howled like demons, and Indians rolled from the tepees shrieking in excitement. Joliet wiped his forehead in relief when the red men came forward with signs of welcome.

These tribesmen were not content to have a short talk with the newcomers. It was not often that they had visitors and they meant to make an occasion of it. A pipe of peace was passed around and long speeches were made by both French and Indians. This was followed by a grand feast of dog meat, porridge, buffalo hump and fish. The big tepee was hot and foul-smelling. Father Marquette had a difficult time with his portion of the banquet, but Joliet ate heartily, smacking his lips and smiling at the chief. That night they remained in the camp, and the following morning were escorted back to the river by a noisy procession of six hundred Indians.

Their calm passage down river was interrupted at the mouth of the Missouri. Here a swirling volume of muddy water ripped into the Mississippi, tossing logs and branches on the churning surface. The canoes bucked like broncos— turning and lurching on the choppy swells. Joliet shouted to the Indians and swung his paddle in windmill sweeps. Father Marquette's lips moved in prayer . . . then Heaven reached down a kindly hand and guided the little craft through the rough waters to placid reaches below the torrent.

After this frightening incident they passed the mouth of

Where the Missouri River joins the Mississippi River, the water was muddy, swift, rough and filled with floating tree branches. The canoes of Joliet and Father Marquette were almost swamped by the rushing torrent.

the Ohio to a land of jungle-like forests that clung to the margins of the river. The pleasant days of the voyage were over. During the hours of light the sun beamed with a furnace heat, and at night thick choking mists hung over their stopping places. Swarms of malarial mosquitoes rose in humming clouds and settled hungrily on the sweating travellers.

At the mouth of the Arkansas they had their most terrifying encounter, when an ugly group of natives gathered in a circle of dugout canoes. They shouted shrill war cries and clutched their bows and arrows in nervous fingers. Father Marquette waved the peace pipe, but this gesture had little effect upon the grim red men. It was a tense situation. Joliet gripped his paddle and set himself for the attack. Then for some unknown reason, a chief silenced the mob and waved the Frenchmen ashore. After that there was a long pow-wow and gradually the Indians became more friendly. They told Joliet that he was only ten days from the sea, but he would be a reckless man to travel on. Warlike Indians who had Spanish guns lived along the coast and they would think nothing of shooting two Frenchmen.

Joliet took this advice seriously. He and Father Marquette realized by this time that the Mississippi did not flow west into the Pacific but kept moving through Spanish lands to the Gulf of Mexico. It would be foolhardy, they thought, to risk the danger of meeting the coastal Indians. They turned about and started the long paddle northward. Father Marquette, suffering from fever, was pale and weak. He was anxious to get back to his mission station.

The trip back upstream was long and tedious, for now they had to fight against the current of the river. At the mouth of the Ohio, Marquette wrote a letter in Latin telling about himself and his missionary work. This he gave to some Indians who said that they traded with European people. By a strange series of adventures this letter reached the English colonies and later was sent to England. Two hundred and twenty years later it was found among some papers in Welbeck Abbey.

Both men were happy when they reached the shelter of the Jesuit mission at Green Bay on Lake Michigan. Marquette, exhausted from the rigours of travel, was content to rest for a period of time. Joliet stayed the winter with his friend, spending most of his time writing the report of their journey. In the spring of 1674 he paddled toward Quebec, probably by way of the Great Lakes. Unfortunately his canoe upset in the Lachine Rapids near Montreal and his three companions were drowned. Lost too, were his own belongings and the precious report he had prepared so carefully.

Nevertheless, Joliet did give an account of the expedition to Count Frontenac and Talon, drawing a rough map from memory. The Governor and Intendant were more than pleased. "Here," they must have said to themselves, "is a waterway from the Great Lakes to the Gulf of Mexico! Here is a new empire for France!"

Father Marquette did not live long after the completion of the famous voyage. He died on Lake Michigan in 1675, and some years later the Indians carried his remains back to the chapel at St. Ignace. Joliet lived for another quarter century after the passing of his friend, and as a reward for his service to New France he was granted the fishing rights about the island of Anticosti in the Gulf of St. Lawrence.

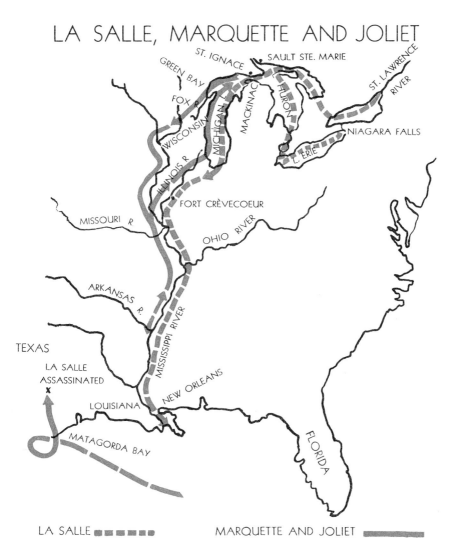

LA SALLE, MARQUETTE AND JOLIET

LA SALLE ▪▪▪▪▪▪   MARQUETTE AND JOLIET ▬▬▬

10 LA SALLE

After the long river journey of Joliet and Marquette Frenchmen began to take an interest in the Mississippi Valley, realizing that here were opportunities for claiming new lands and for opening additional areas for the fur trade.

Indians on the shores of Lake Erie chattered among themselves and pointed in amazement across the water. "Big canoe! Big canoe!" they shouted.

To the red men it was an astounding sight. There on the lazy roll of the lake rode a forty-five ton vessel, her white sails round and taut in the breeze. Foam broke away from her blunt nose and long swells trailed behind her high stern. Here was the *Griffon*, the first ship to sail the Great Lakes above Niagara Falls. Little wonder that the Indians chattered and pointed.

On the deck of the *Griffon* stood René Robert Cavalier, Sieur de la Salle, a handsome Frenchman with sparkling eyes and long curly hair that hung down to his shoulders. With a smile on his face he turned to his Italian friend, Henry Tonti. "Well, Henry," he said, "we're off on the greatest adventure of our lives. Think of it, man! The King's permission to trade on the Mississippi, and a right to explore the river to its mouth! We'll make a fortune in furs and give France lands she has never dreamed of. We'll build a line of forts down the length of the river, and hold the heart of a continent."

Tonti smiled, but shook his head. "Maybe," he said, "but so much can go wrong—Indian attacks, English raiders, bad weather, fever and shipwreck. Don't forget too, that the traders of New France have no love for you. They are jealous of your high standing with the Governor and the King."

It was the year 1679. The *Griffon* sailed on through the Detroit River, Lake St. Clair, River St. Clair, Lake Huron and then into Lake Michigan. Near Green Bay they met some of La Salle's men who had been sent ahead the previous year to trade with the Illinois Indians. It was a noisy, joyful meeting and one that called for a celebration. The trading canoes were filled with heavy packs of dark furs. La Salle stroked the sleek pelts and chuckled in satisfaction. These would help him repay the money he had borrowed in New France.

The furs were loaded onto the *Griffon,* and the ship was ordered back to Niagara. As La Salle watched its sails grow smaller in the distance, he did not know that he was seeing his vessel for the last time. Months later Indians reported that they had seen the *Griffon* in a fierce storm, tossing like a stricken phantom on the black waters . . . and then she had disappeared.

La Salle's hard luck had just begun. Still unaware of the loss of the vessel, he went to the Illinois River and there built two forts. One of these was called Crèvecoeur (Fort Heartbreak), and time proved that it was a very apt name. Some time later La Salle made the long journey back to Montreal, leaving Henry Tonti in charge. La Salle, quite rightly, had every confidence in this remarkable Italian, who had lost his hand in battle and replaced it with a metal hook. "Tonti of the Silver Hand" the Indians called him, and they watched in awe as he wielded his hook to strike a man or rip open a fish.

Once back in Montreal, La Salle was shocked by the news that the *Griffon* was lost. Added to this was the startling report that a vessel carrying his trading goods from France had disappeared at sea! These staggering losses were enough to make a man give up the trading business, but La Salle was not an ordinary man. With a shrug of his shoulder he started making more plans. After borrowing as much money as he could, he bought supplies, hired men, and started back to the Illinois country.

At Fort Crèvecoeur, he was faced with additional tragedy. His post had been wiped out by the Iroquois and his men were gone. There was no sign of Henry Tonti, so that La Salle took for granted that his friend was dead.

Still determined to make a success of the fur trade in the Mississippi Valley, he went again to Montreal, secured more supplies, and returned to the west. During the autumn of 1680, he reached Mackinac and on arrival, started in surprise as if he had seen a ghost. There stood Henry Tonti! The two men shouted aloud and rushed toward each other.

The following year they set up more trading posts and held important meetings with the Indians. By the winter of 1682 they were ready to start the long-awaited dash to the distant mouth of the Mississippi. During February, La Salle, Tonti, thirty Frenchmen and a band of Indians set their canoes in the water and paddled southward. Just as Louis Joliet, nineteen years before, had thrilled to the beauties of the Mississippi, so did La Salle. He marvelled at the fine timber, the fertile soil, the flocks of birds, the grazing deer and the shaggy buffalo. They passed the Ohio, the Missouri and the point near the mouth of the Arkansas where Joliet and Marquette had turned back. On they went, sweating in the heat and brushing away a fog of mosquitoes. At last, three months and two days after the start of the journey, they passed low swampy banks and came to the open sea.

A great mystery had been solved. Here was final proof that the Mississippi flowed south into the Gulf of Mexico. It

At the mouth of the Mississippi River, La Salle raised a flag and claimed the land for France. This district he called Louisiana in honour of King Louis. What important city was later founded there by the French?

was the same river that Hernando de Soto had seen—the same river that had gulped the Spaniard's thin body in the black of night.

La Salle, bubbling over with the success of the expedition, landed and raised the flag, claiming the whole valley of the

Mississippi in the name of France. To this new French Empire he gave the name Louisiana in honour of his King—a name still held by the state at the mouth of the river.

Filled with magnificent dreams, La Salle hurried back to Quebec and on to France. Before King Louis, he reported his explorations and described the wealth of the spacious lands in the core of America. Eagerly he poured out his plans and his hopes for the new country. Shrewdly he pointed out to the monarch that if France did not take possession of the valley, England or Spain would most certainly do so. A French colony, he said, should be founded at the mouth of the Mississippi and a line of forts constructed up the whole course of the river. By this plan the English could be prevented from spreading westward from their colonies along the eastern coast of America.

The King was impressed by the explorer's eagerness and granted royal permission for the founding of a settlement. La Salle left France in July, 1684, with four ships and a group of colonists and soldiers. The sailing vessels crossed the Atlantic, turned the tip of Florida and glided on toward the Mississippi. La Salle was happy and the colonists talked brightly of their future homes on the southern shores.

If ever a man deserved good fortune at this point it was La Salle, but the evil shadow of his hard luck stayed with him. The squadron missed the mouth of the river and landed in Texas, four hundred miles west of the goal. That was alarming in itself, but nothing compared to the disaster which came with the wrecking of the vessel which held most of their stores and equipment. There was nothing to do but make the best of the situation. A settlement and fort were set up at Matagorda Bay, and the settlers resented their dangerous position.

Several attempts were made to find the river mouth, but these were hopeless, heartbreaking affairs. At last, in January

1687, La Salle left the coast with sixteen men, hoping to reach Quebec. The men pushed northward through Texas, making slow progress and losing faith in the success of the attempt. Had La Salle been more kindly and less demanding, the spirit and courage of the men might have been raised. He himself was determined and tireless, and he expected his men to be the same. His hungry followers grumbled and chafed at the sharp commands. Then came the end . . . a musket roared . . . a bullet flew . . . warm blood spurted . . . the French leader gasped out his life on the prairie. Like Hernando Pizarro and Henry Hudson, La Salle died at the hands of his own men.

La Salle's forlorn little colony disappeared, but the efforts and sacrifices of the great adventurer had not been in vain, for the French came back to the southern shores and founded New Orleans, a romantic and colourful settlement.

Thanks to the energy of her explorers and traders, France now claimed all the land that lay in a sweeping curve from the Gulf of Mexico to the Gulf of St. Lawrence. Could she hold this vast territory against her rivals, the Spanish and the English?

11 RADISSON AND GROSEILLIERS

It was to be expected that the wandering fur traders of New France should eventually reach the shores of Hudson Bay, but it was strange that this activity should lead to the founding of a great English trading company.

The Governor of New France read the crumpled letter, and then puffed loudly through his whiskers. He passed the letter to a clerk. "These young rascals want to trade in furs on a Northern Sea. Tell them that they have my permission, providing that they take two of my men with them and hand over half the profits of the expedition. If this arrangment is not accepted, they must not depart on any mission to the north country!"

When Pierre Radisson and his brother-in-law, Medard Groseilliers received the Governor's reply, they were furious. "Imagine," shouted Radisson, "he wants half the profits! We take all the risks, while he sits in comfort at home. We would be fools to accept such a plan!"

One dark night, some time later, the two woodsmen slipped silently from their home, walked cautiously across the settlement of Three Rivers, opened the gate in the stockade and vanished into the blackness. After joining a wandering band of Indians, they made their way to the deep forests beyond Lake Superior. There they lived with the Crees, hunting and roaming the woods. Life with the Indians was not strange to Radisson, for as a boy he had been captured by the Iroquois and held prisoner for several years. In the Superior country the two men met the Assiniboine Indians, who spoke of the salt Sea of the North.

Radisson's records of their travels are not clear and still remain a puzzle to historians. However, it is probable that the two fur traders moved southward to the headwaters of the Mississippi River, and then journeyed through rich fur lands, far north of Lake Superior. Radisson claims that they reached Hudson Bay, but of this we are not sure. In his writings he describes an arduous voyage down a river—perhaps the Albany or the Moose. The weather was still cold, floating ice slid along in the current, rocks along the shores were wet and slippery, and damp winds chilled the paddlers. As if this were not enough, they came to a region of desolate swamps where rotted trees had fallen, lacing the shallow waters with a treacherous network of stumps, limbs and branches. It was a frightful place in which to move the fragile canoes, but on they went, wading in the frigid waters and pushing the light craft around the many obstacles. Shivering, stumbling, slipping and falling they advanced painfully. Radisson sprained his ankle and suffered agonies in the watery trek.

Whether or not they reached the sea at this time matters little; the important fact is that they conceived the idea of building trading posts at the mouths of rivers flowing into Hudson Bay. This was a dream they held for the future.

During the summer of 1660 Radisson and Groseilliers made a dramatic arrival below the heights of Quebec, with hundreds of Indians and a fleet of canoes loaded with beaver skins.

Radisson and Groseilliers travelled into the unknown country north of Lake Superior. What great fur company was founded as a result of their daring travels?

Radisson looked at the settlement and stroked his beard. "I wonder what the Governor will say?" he murmured.

That question was soon answered. The Governor was furious with the two adventurers. He fined them heavily for their disobedience, took away most of their pelts, and left them with a miserable remainder for their dangerous expedition.

Groseilliers hurried to France and appealed to the King for a return of their furs, but it was of no use. Friends of the Governor persuaded the King that no wrong had been done to the traders.

Back again in Three Rivers, Groseilliers reported to his brother-in-law what had taken place in France. Radisson fumed in rage. "If France won't help us, England will!" he roared.

In the summer of 1665, they sailed from the British colonies on an English ship, but even on the high seas they could not avoid adventure. The vessel was attacked and sunk by a Dutch pirate, and the two men were put ashore in Spain. They were penniless, but by selling some clothes they managed to reach London, England. Surprising as it may seem, King Charles II received the wanderers at his court and listened to their vivid stories of exploration in the northern woods. Pleased with their accounts, his majesty generously ordered that the Frenchmen be paid forty shillings a week during that year.

Radisson and Groseilliers were the talk of London, but were known by the simpler names of Mr. Radishes and Mr. Gooseberry. A group of courtiers became interested in the woodsmen and entertained them to lavish dinners at inns and coffee houses. Through a cloud of smoke from long-stemmed pipes, the handsome gallants in their velvet coats listened with awe to the sparkling stories of Radisson.

Events soon passed the stage of roast beef dinners and tales of adventure, for in the spring of 1668 two ships left England, with Radisson aboard the *Eaglet* and Groseilliers aboard the *Nonsuch*. Radisson's ship was disabled and the disappointed Frenchman was forced to return. However, Groseilliers sailed on to Hudson Bay and in the following spring returned with a cargo of furs that caused English eyes to pop with amazement.

The group of noble and wealthy men who had supplied ships and men for the voyage lost no time in forming a company to continue the fur trade on the northern shores of Canada. King Charles, in May 1670, scrawled his name on a large sheet of parchment, thus signing the charter granted to *The Governor and Company of Adventurers Trading into Hudson's Bay.* This was the birth of the famous Hudson's

Bay Company, an organization which played such a vital part in the development of Canada.

As King Charles signed the charter, he had little idea how much land and power he was giving to the gallants of his court. According to charter, the new company was to own the land and have trading rights in all the territory drained by rivers flowing into Hudson Bay. That really included a land mass stretching from the Rockies to Labrador. With the sweep of a pen an empire had fallen into the hands of the merchant-noblemen.

Soon frigates were going back and forth between England and Hudson Bay, carrying supplies one way and furs the other. Beaver hats had become fashionable in Europe, so the pelts of the beaver were eagerly purchased. Profits were high and business was good. Forts appeared about the margin of Hudson Bay, and the Indians paddled hundreds of miles for the precious goods at the posts.

Radisson and Groseilliers were in the centre of this exciting activity, but after a time they became dissatisfied and quarrelled with the company over their share of the profits. Suddenly they left England, returned to New France and began trading in the Bay under the French flag. Here with supreme audacity they captured two English trading vessels and sailed them back to Quebec. Once again they met the wrath of the French Governor. The British ships were freed and the two adventurers were ordered off to France to report on their crimes. After this unpleasant period, Groseilliers, disgusted with the fur trade, gave up and retired to Three Rivers.

Radisson, a rebel at heart, did not give up but went back with the Hudson's Bay Company and rose to the position of Superintendent of Trade. In spite of this promising situation, he was a man with a price on his head. The French King offered "fifty pistoles" to anyone who would capture the treasonous fur trader.

No man claimed the reward. In later years Radisson lived on in London, almost a forgotten person, struggling along on a meager salary. Through the gray fogs that hung over the chimney pots he saw visions of forest trails, Indian canoes, trading posts, fast frigates and piles of beaver skins.

The old trailmaker died in London during the spring of 1710, and his lonely widow was forced to live on charity. It was a pathetic ending for a valiant man whose dreams had formed the Hudson's Bay Company.

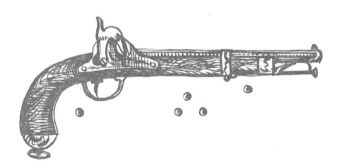

12   HENRY HUDSON

After the voyage of John Cabot, England continued to take an interest in the New World, but like France she did not establish colonies until long after Spain was settled in the southern regions of the Americas. British seamen such as Frobisher, Davis and Baffin sailed Arctic waters in search of a North West Passage to the East. In 1607, one year before Champlain founded Quebec, the English established a colony in Virginia which grew and prospered. Then, in 1610, a British ship made its way along the northern coast of America and entered Hudson Bay.

A stout innkeeper in Old London poked vigorously at the coals in a stone fireplace and then turned to smile at several gentlemen sitting about in oak chairs.

"Did ye know that Henry Hudson be back in England?" he asked.

The men looked interested, and one of them asked, "And who might Henry Hudson be?"

The innkeeper, quite ready to talk at any time, took a pinch of snuff and cleared his throat. "Henry Hudson, sir, be an excellent navigator in the service of the English Muscovy Company. Quite recently 'e undertook to make a long voyage across the North Pole to China."

"Across the North Pole?" demanded a thin, old lawyer. "The man must be crazy!"

"Maybe so," said the innkeeper, "but, begging your pardon, sir, 'e is a good navigator nevertheless. 'E sailed along the coast of Greenland through bitter waters until 'e was blocked by a great mass of ice. Then 'e swung eastward and reached Spitzbergen before 'e came back to England."

"A silly waste of ships and money," snorted the lawyer. "English seamen would be wise to give up this foolish notion of a passage to the East."

"Maybe so, sir," said the innkeeper quietly, "but as ye know, Englishmen be stubborn fellows. I daresay we'll be hearing more of this Henry Hudson."

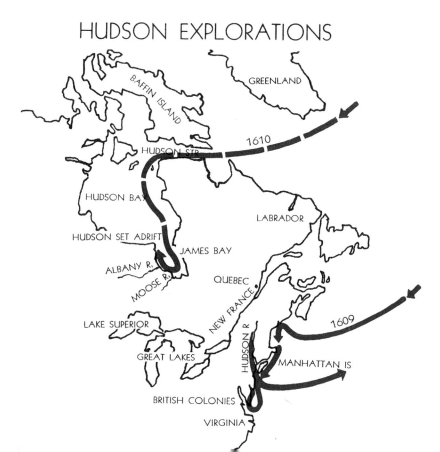

HUDSON EXPLORATIONS

The innkeeper was right, for England did hear a great deal more about the navigator Henry Hudson.

In 1608 the Muscovy Company sent Hudson northward again to see if there was a navigable route along the coast of Russia, but this voyage too was a failure. The ship rounded Norway and made good progress as far as Novaya Zemlya off Russian shores, but turned back at this point. It may have been that the crew mutinied and refused to go on. While he was an excellent navigator and a courageous explorer, Hudson did not know how to handle men. It was this weakness that later cost him his life.

Hudson's third voyage was in the service of the Dutch East India Company. During this expedition he set for himself the goal of finding a western route to the East. A letter received from Virginia led Hudson to believe that a wide waterway lay in that part of North America. Having reached the eastern coast, he explored the shores from Nova Scotia to Virginia, and during the course of his sailing he found Manhattan Island and the mouth of a river now named the Hudson. This waterway interested him, so he turned the bow of his ship upstream. The navigator and his crew watched the shores closely and stopped from time to time to talk with friendly Indians. To Hudson's disappointment the river became narrower and narrower, and finally the ship could go no farther. This, Hudson realized, was not the passage he sought.

After returning to Europe, Hudson left the service of the Dutch East India Company and was employed by an English group of merchants who were interested in finding a North West Passage across the top of America. The company secured a tough little vessel, the *Discovery*, which had already been to the Arctic seas with an English explorer, George Waymouth. Waymouth had reported finding the mouth of a wide strait lying between Baffin Island and Labrador. This information together with the records of other voyagers led the English company to believe that there was a good chance of finding a passage across the northern seas.

In April, 1610, Hudson set off in the *Discovery* and with little difficulty he found the strait mentioned in the log book of George Waymouth. Unfortunately, Hudson's crew, as on his former voyages, was restless and troublesome. Much of the uneasiness was caused by an untrustworthy mate, Robert Juet, and a second man, Henry Greene. As the *Discovery* made its way through the passage now called Hudson Strait, the seamen became frightened by the desolate, barren shores. They imagined all sorts of dangers, and finally refused to go any farther into the dreary wastes. With great difficulty Hudson managed to reduce their fears by explaining the purpose of the voyage and the great rewards that would come with success. Slowly the *Discovery* moved westward through strong currents and floating pans of ice. Jagged black rocks rose through the mists and seabirds screamed above the breakers.

On August 3, the *Discovery* broke through a passage five miles wide and faced an open sea. Hudson was jubilant with the great space of water stretching away to the west and the south. He was fully satisfied that he had come to the shores of the Pacific Ocean. Joyfully he turned the bow of his vessel southward, but as the weeks went by, the coastline remained cold and forbidding. Worse still, the days became shorter and shorter and the weather much colder. Floating ice made its appearance in the waters.

Hudson's worst fears were realized when the *Discovery*'s southward passage was stopped by solid land. We know now that the ship had run the whole length of Hudson Bay, into James Bay and had reached the tip of that basin. Hudson realized with alarm that he was not on the Pacific, but in a

During the long voyage from England to Hudson Bay the little sailing ship, "Discovery," sailed along cold and gloomy shores which frightened the sailors, and started them thinking of mutiny.

great basin that thrust itself deeply into the northern coast of America.

The crew, terrified by the prospect of spending a winter in that desolate place, protested loudly. Robert Juet, the mate, appears to have taken a leading part in the protest, for Hudson put Juet on trial and then took his rank from him. A new mate, Robert Bylot, was put in his place.

The *Discovery* was frozen in near the southern tip of James Bay. Winter was a terrible experience for Hudson and his men, as the ship had not been outfitted for such an emergency. Food, heavy clothing and fuel were all in short supply. The seamen were wet, cold and hungry. They managed to kill a few ptarmigan, and when spring came they shot a few ducks and caught some fish, but these were not enough to supply their needs.

It was not until June 12, 1611, that they were able to move the ship among the cakes of ice. By this time Hudson had removed Bylot as mate and appointed the quartermaster, John King, an ignorant sailor quite unfit for this post. The seamen were seething with discontentment and fear. Rations were low. Everyone thought of death by starvation.

Open revolt broke out on board the *Discovery* twelve days after she was free from the ice. The mutineers were led by three ruthless men—Henry Greene, Robert Juet and William Wilson. Acting swiftly, the rebels seized Hudson together with his son, the mate and four sailors, two of whom were ill. They were all placed in a small boat tied to the stern of the *Discovery*. The alarmed prisoners were told that they were being placed in the shallop only until the food stores of the ship were examined. It soon became apparent, however, that no such simple plan was in the making. Horrified by the heartless action of the mutiny leaders, the ship's carpenter protested loudly. Gathering up his tools, a musket, a few kettles and a little food, this heroic man went over the side of the *Discovery* and joined the pathetic prisoners in the shallop.

The quick slash of a knife cut the tow rope, and the *Discovery* drew away, her bow pointed to open water. As the mutineers looked back, the tiny boat became a lonely speck on the horizon.

A strange fate brought the *Discovery* back to England, but not one of the mutiny leaders lived to enjoy the arrival. Henry Greene and William Wilson were killed by Eskimos on Hudson Strait; Robert Juet died on the Atlantic. Only a miserable remnant of the crew reached England alive, and from these Europe learned the story of the amazing expedition. By very good fortune Hudson's log book and charts passed unharmed through the adventures of the voyage, and these records caused great interest among merchants and geographers.

It is most peculiar that the surviving members of the voyage were not hanged for their crimes. Actually they were brought to trial and then set free. Their knowledge of Hudson's explorations was considered too valuable to be wasted on the gallows. At least two of the rascals lived to take part in another expedition to the Arctic commanded by Thomas Button.

Although Henry Hudson perished somewhere in the James Bay Region, his name is still very much alive today: Hudson Bay, Hudson Strait, Hudson River and the Hudson's Bay Company remind us of this great explorer. His discoveries opened a new passage for others to follow, and they gave England a sound claim for lands which now make up more than half of Canada.

13 DANIEL DU LHUT
COUREUR DE BOIS

At the time when Count Frontenac was Governor of New France, there were five or six hundred reckless young Frenchmen roaming the wilderness, living with the Indians and trading cheap gadgets for furs and skins.

These gay young blades lived a colourful but dangerous life paddling the lakes and rivers, tramping the forests and hunting on the prairies. They let their black whiskers grow into long beards, dressed in greasy buckskins, slept in Indian huts and ate their food with scalping knives. Many of them took Indian wives and gave up civilization entirely; some sank to the level of savages, torturing and killing their enemies with a ferocity greater than that of the red men.

These lean, hard woodsmen were called *coureurs de bois*, meaning "runners of the woods."

Fur trading done by the coureurs de bois was strictly against the laws of New France, since large trading companies were given full rights to fur trade by the French king. Nevertheless, these bold adventurers continued to trade with the Indians, travelling wherever they willed. When they secured a cargo of furs, they smuggled them into Montreal and sold

93

them secretly, or took them south to the English towns of Albany or Boston where the pelts sold at high prices.

Such impudent trading, of course, caused howls of rage from the company traders, who sent angry letters of protest to the King. The monarch was very much annoyed to think that young Frenchmen were ignoring royal orders, and, as a result, he commanded that the coureurs de bois be fined, imprisoned or sentenced as galley slaves. It was very simple to issue such orders, but not so easy to carry them out. Who in New France had the time or the money to chase the rascals through a thousand miles of forest? The coureurs de bois calmly went on with their unlawful trading. Some were caught and thrown into prison, but most of these had powerful friends in New France—the captives' fines were paid, and they returned to the woods.

The greatest of all the coureurs de bois was a nobleman, Daniel Greysolon, Sieur du Lhut, who at one time had been an officer in the bodyguard of King Louis of France. Becoming tired of the ceremonious life in the palace of the King, he had sailed to New France and settled in Montreal where he built a large house with a beautiful garden facing on the St. Lawrence.

Du Lhut was not satisfied for long with this quiet life, so he sold his home, took to a canoe, and for the next twenty-nine years lived in the wilderness. On his first journey to the West he made his way along the old canoe route, up the Ottawa, across to Lake Huron and on to Mackinac where Father Marquette had lived and worked. There he found an important trading centre occupied by two hundred French and six thousand Indians.

After a short stay he went on to the land of the Dakota Indians, and it was there that his amazing career among the red men began. In his dealings with the Indians, he kept two aims in mind: one, to keep peace among the tribes; and the other, to win friends for New France. In gaining both of these goals, he was remarkably successful. Unlike many of the coureurs de bois, who became mere renegades, Du Lhut remained a true gentleman, and it was this fact which enabled him to keep the good will of the natives. He travelled hundreds of miles through the tribal lands, and was well known to thousands of the red men.

During the summer of 1680 he was moving through what is now the mid-western part of the United States, when he received news that a Frenchman was being held captive by a tribe of Indians on the Mississippi River. Travelling swiftly

Although Du Lhut was held in prison for illegal fur trading, he had dinner each evening with Count Frontenac. Here Frontenac listens as Du Lhut describes some fur trading adventure.

with a small party, he reached the Indian camp and there he found a thin starved priest, Father Hennepin. With cool daring, Du Lhut faced two thousand Sioux Indians and demanded that the priest be released. It was a daring move, and one that brought the admiration of the warriors. The chiefs apologized for holding Father Hennepin and promised that the priest would be set free. Then blue smoke curled from pipes of peace and a great feast was prepared.

So it was that after three years of travel and exploration in the southwest, Du Lhut returned to Montreal with Father Hennepin. New France was by no means grateful to the adventurer for his efforts in her behalf—Du Lhut was arrested and put in prison. It was a strange captivity! Count Frontenac held a secret sympathy for the bold wanderer and had dinner with him each evening in the vice-regal chateau in Quebec!

Eventually the captive was forgiven his sins and was hired by the government to broaden the fur trade in the west. He set up a trading post where the City of Fort William now stands, and to that point he attracted tribes who lived hundreds of miles away in the forests and on the prairies. Year after year he continued in the service of France, trading, exploring, and leading military expeditions against the English and hostile Indians. He journeyed thousands of miles, by canoe in summer, by snowshoe in winter, and few men have equalled his record of hard, continuous travel.

When the Iroquois swooped down on the little settlement of Lachine, near Montreal, and massacred the French settlers, it was Du Lhut who took first revenge on the enemy. With thirty coureurs de bois he paddled up the Ottawa, met a party of Iroquois and defeated them in a short skirmish.

Although Du Lhut spent a long period in the fur trade, he never became a wealthy man, for he was interested only in exploration, adventure, and the spread of French power in America.

After twenty-nine years of strenuous life in the fur trade he gave up his command of Fort Detroit and retired to Quebec. Although he was not yet sixty years of age, he was bent, wrinkled and suffering from gout. Nevertheless on pleasant days he walked the streets of the town in a fine brown suit, a scarlet cape, a wide plumed hat and carried a cane with a silver handle. He looked what he had always been—a gallant nobleman.

Daniel Du Lhut, "King of the Coureurs de Bois," passed away in Montreal in February, 1710, and at his burial he was honoured by the greatest men in New France. No Frenchman had been more loyal to his King, nor more determined in promoting the good of his country, or more admired by scattered tribes of Indians.

His name still survives on the map of North America, since the city of Duluth, at the tip of Lake Superior, was named in his honour.

14 LA VÉRENDRYE

The French, seeking new lands and new fur country, had explored the Great Lakes, reached Hudson Bay, and had pushed down the Mississippi River to the Gulf of Mexico. It was only a matter of time until they were to discover the vast unknown plains which we now call the prairies. The first important exploration in the west was accomplished, not by a single man, but by a family of pathfinders whose name is famous in North American history.

I

The governor of Three Rivers lived in a low rambling house outside the walls of the French settlement. Although an important man, he was not a wealthy one and his family certainly did not live in great luxury. Among the ten children of the family was a sturdy, robust boy, Pierre Gaultier de La Vérendrye, who soon learned to handle a musket and watch for raiding bands of Iroquois.

At that time boys entered their life's work when still quite young. Pierre was just twelve years of age when he was considered old enough to enter the army as a cadet. Seven years later, he was marching southward in the dead of winter toward an English settlement in Massachusetts. One bitter, cold morning the French and Indians slid quietly over a wooden stockade, gripped their guns, shrieked a warwhoop and rushed toward the dark cabins. After the vicious attack was over, weeping prisoners were driven through the snow away from burning homes and the bodies of their loved ones. To such a stern life as this, the young Frenchman was trained.

That was just the beginning of a military career that took him to Acadia and later to the battlefields of Europe. When he was twenty-six years of age, he left the army and returned to the St. Lawrence to enter the fur trade. Even as a small boy at Three Rivers, La Vérendrye had heard Indian tales of the Lake Superior fur lands and of a salt water sea that stretched beyond the western plains. Just how far west the salt sea lay, no one knew. It was the same sea that had shone in the dreams of Cartier, Champlain, Joliet, La Salle and a host of others. These stories fascinated La Vérendrye and roused in him a feverish desire to see the unknown lands beyond Superior. Life as a fur trader provided the excuse to travel in these lands.

La Vérendrye married a French girl and in the course of time four sons arrived in the family. These lads grew into strong vigorous youths who joined their father in business as soon as they were able to do so. Later they were to help greatly in his exploration.

By 1726, La Vérendrye was in charge of an important post on Lake Nipigon, north of Lake Superior. There he met a wrinkled old chief, Ochagach, who told colourful stories of his travels along a prairie river which emptied into a lake drained by a second river flowing westward into the sea. The chief said that he had not reached salt water, but other Indians had informed him that he was very close to it. To make the description more vivid, Ochagach drew for La Vérendrye a map of the prairie waterways on a sheet of birchbark.

Excited by this information, La Vérendrye hurried back

to Quebec and asked permission to lead an expedition into the western region. He hoped that France would provide him with some men and would pay the expenses of the journey. The Governor was pleased with the idea and wrote to the King, but the monarch was not feeling generous at the time. He said that La Vérendrye might go west and have full rights to the fur trade there, but he must pay all costs of the expeditions himself.

La Vérendrye was disappointed. He realized that he must borrow money, set up a line of trading posts, and use the profits of the fur trade to pay the costs of exploration. There was no other way to reach his goal. The merchants of Montreal were not interested in a mere journey of discovery, but trade in beaver skins . . . that was different! Under those conditions they were only too eager to supply him with canoes, soldiers, voyageurs, provisions, trade goods and other equipment. They struck a hard bargain with the impatient explorer, and it was not until later that La Vérendrye realized how difficult was his position.

During the summer of 1731 the expedition set off, and among the party were La Vérendrye's three sons, Jean Baptiste, Pierre, François, and his nephew, La Jemeraye. The warm months were nearly over when they reached the spot where the city of Fort William now stands. Half of the party remained there for the winter and the other half, under La Jemeraye, went on to Rainy River, built a fort and traded with the Indians. That was the first post in the long line that La Vérendrye hoped to spread on toward the distant sea. As soon as he could move in the spring, the explorer pushed on to Lake of the Woods and on a point running out into the lake a second fort was built. The following winter La Vérendrye's eldest son, Jean, and a few tough woodsmen travelled by snowshoes four hundred and fifty miles to Lake Winnipeg and set up a third fort.

LA VÉRENDRYE EXPLORATIONS

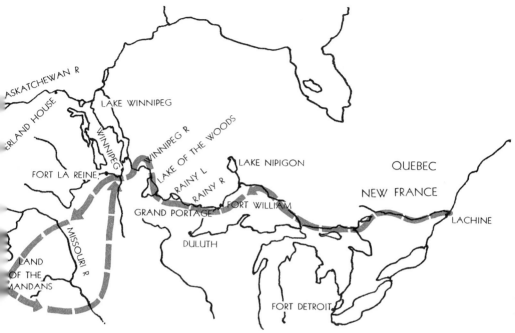

In spite of this rapid progress, La Vérendrye was discouraged. Trading was good, but the cost of keeping his men and forts was very high. All of his own money was gone. The merchants in Montreal demanded more beaver skins and refused to forward more supplies to the west. If only the King had given him a few men and allowed him to explore swiftly without the hindrance of the fur trade! What quick movements he could have made!

There was nothing to do but return to Montreal and talk with the merchants. Once back on the St. Lawrence, he described the posts he had built, the endless herds of buffalo, the wealth of the furs and the tribes eager for trade. The red men, he said, were quite willing to stop trading with the English posts on Hudson Bay if they could reach French forts on the prairies. La Vérendrye's moving appeal had its effect, for once again the merchants outfitted him with trading supplies and provisions for his forts. La Vérendrye, leaving for the West, was pleased that he could go on with his exploration, but was disturbed by the fact that he owed the merchants more money than ever.

La Vérendrye was like La Salle—a man doomed to live in the shadow of misfortune. Pushing ahead of his supply canoes, he reached Lake of the Woods to find that his nephew had died, and that his men in the fort were in a starving condition. A small group, led by Jean, was hurried off in the direction of the supply canoes to secure food for the fort. Part way across the lake they stopped to rest on the shore of an island. They were smoking and talking idly, when a hundred Sioux warriors leaped from behind the trees, shooting arrows as they came. The Frenchmen not felled by the first volley, snatched their guns and returned the fire, but, surrounded as they were, they could not defend themselves. Tossing their muskets aside, they leaped into the lake and began swimming frantically toward a distant island. The Sioux braves watched in satisfaction as one by one the dark heads sank beneath the rippling waters.

The loss of his nephew, La Jemeraye, and his son, Jean, was a terrible blow to La Vérendrye, a blow from which he never recovered. Nevertheless, his determination to reach the Western Sea was still strong. He went on with his work.

II

From the tribes of the prairies—Chippewayans, Crees and Assiniboines—he heard of an Indian people, the Mandans, who lived to the south and the west. The Mandans were a strange tribe, the Indians said, for they had white skins, wore armour, rode horses and lived in walled towns. These accounts were so enticing that La Vérendrye decided to travel to the Mandan villages and see these natives for himself. Starting off with a few men including his two sons, he passed the place where Winnipeg now stands and went on to the location of present day Portage La Prairie. There he erected another fort and named it Fort La Reine in honour of his Queen. When this duty was completed, he continued his trek toward the land of the Mandans.

A few days after leaving Fort La Reine the party arrived at an Assiniboine village and was entertained by the Indians. Following the usual speeches and feast, the tribesmen calmly announced that they were going with the Frenchmen to the Mandan country. La Vérendrye was taken aback by this unexpected development, but he could not afford to offend the Assiniboines by refusing such a generous offer. The next morning they left the village with six hundred Indians, including warriors, hunters, scouts, squaws and children. La Vérendrye smiled as he watched the long procession that stretched across the prairies.

Late in the autumn they came to the Mandan territory and were warmly welcomed by a friendly people who dressed in the hides of buffalo. La Vérendrye was surprised to find that these Indians looked very much like the Assiniboines, and he realized then that the stories about white-skinned Mandans had been greatly exaggerated. The village they reached, however, was no disappointment—a massive wooden stockade and a deep moat completely surrounded one hundred and thirty cabins laid out in neat streets. It was the finest Indian settlement that the Frenchmen had ever seen.

The Mandans were not so warm in their greetings to the Assiniboines as they were in their welcome to the French— so many visitors could eat tremendous quantities of food. Shrewdly, the Mandans spread the rumour that a large body of Sioux was approaching to attack the village, and this ruse had its desired effect. The Assiniboines broke camp and hurried back home, anxious to avoid battle with their hated enemies.

La Vérendrye and his French companions remained with the Mandans for several weeks after the departure of their Indian friends. They questioned the villagers about the Western Seas, but secured very little new information. The Indians, however, spoke of other tribes living farther to the southwest who rode horses and travelled to the mountains. The year was almost over when the French party said good-bye to their gracious hosts and started back to Fort La Reine.

La Vérendrye hoped to make a return trip to the Mandan country the following spring, but found that his duties in the fur trade would not permit him to do so. In 1742, he was still

The La Vérendrye boys travelled southwest across the prairies with the Bow Indians until they saw a range of mountains in the distance. They were very pleased, for they thought they were coming to the western sea.

too occupied to go, but he did send off his two sons with orders to reach the Western Sea if they possibly could.

The sons and two other Frenchmen made a quick trip to the Mandan villages, secured several guides and went on toward the southwest. Everywhere they went, they were treated with generosity by the Indians, and by good fortune, they arrived in a village of the Bow Indians at a time when the warriors were about to start on a raid into the land of the Snake Indians. This journey, the Bows said, would take them to mountains from which the Western Sea could be viewed. Rejoicing at their good fortune, the Frenchmen joined the huge column which consisted of more than two thousand braves, squaws and children. This war party was different from any the La Vérendrye brothers had ever seen, for the Bows had hundreds of horses which carried warriors and dragged heavy travois across the plains.

Astride wiry spotted ponies, the Frenchmen trotted along in the vivid procession, across the dry prairies to the southwest. After weeks of tiresome travel, they finally came in sight of a range of mountains, whose snow-capped peaks gleamed in the morning sun. To the explorers the first glimpse of the distant range was a thrilling sight. They were impatient to reach the mountains, climb the peaks and look westward on the salty seas. It was impossible for them to know that the ocean lay hundreds of miles beyond those purple foothills.

Then arose one of those strange situations which were not uncommon in Indian warfare. The Bow Indians discovered that the Snakes had retreated rather than face their enemies. Instead of being pleased by this move, the Bows were thrown into confusion, and they themselves beat a quick retreat in spite of the entreaties of their chief.

Realizing that it would be dangerous to advance alone, the La Vérendrye brothers regretfully turned back with the retiring Bows. Later they left the column and headed for the

Missouri River to explore the land there. After arriving at the river, they met the Cherry Indians, who, like other red men, accepted the Frenchmen with kindness and courtesy.

On the west bank of the river the La Vérendryes buried a lead plate bearing their names and the royal arms of the King. One hundred and seventy years later, in 1913, an American school girl stooped to pick from the dirt the same little metal plate which had claimed the prairies for the crown of France.

Swinging northward from the land of the Cherry tribe, they rode to the Mandan villages and then pushed on toward Fort La Reine with a group of Assiniboines. One year and eighty-four days after the beginning of the journey they came in sight of their father's post. La Vérendrye rushed to meet his sons as he saw them approaching. It was a happy reunion, for the father had been deeply concerned by the long absence of his two sons.

While the brothers had been exploring, La Vérendrye had built more forts and extended the fur trade, but trouble was brewing in New France. Rival fur traders, jealous of his western rights, were making bitter complaints and false charges against La Vérendrye.

The selfish schemes of the eastern traders won in the end; the La Vérendrye family was commanded to leave the prairies and return to Quebec. This was a cruel rebuff to a gallant Frenchman who had tried so hard to reach the Western Sea.

After the disheartened father and sons left the prairies, another Frenchman was placed in charge of trade and exploration, but the new man made little progress. It soon became clear to the rulers of New France that the La Vérendrye family had done a magnificent work in opening the West for French trade.

When La Vérendrye was sixty-four years of age, he was called by the Governor to take up once more the task of exploring the prairies. In spite of his age, he gladly began preparations for a westward expedition to be launched in the spring of 1750. In the hustle and bustle of collecting men, canoes and equipment, he took ill and died.

Neither La Vérendrye nor his sons reached the salty seas beyond the mountains, but in their determined efforts to do so, they had explored much of what is now western Canada and the United States of America.

15 THE BUFFALO HUNTERS

*Three wild animals in particular had important effects upon the
history of North America . . . the beaver, the buffalo and the sea-
otter. These were the animals that set ships flying across the
waters, and men scurrying through the forests and over the plains;
these the animals for which men explored, travelled, fought and
died.*

*Here is the story of the big, hump-back beast that roamed the
prairies, in dark herds that stretched for miles across the dry brown
grasses.*

The rumble of ten thousand hoofs shook the ground, half-
naked Indians whooped shrilly, coureurs de bois in dirty
buckskins laughed through their black beards, and over the
whole scene hung a choking dust that dimmed the sunlight.
Stampeding buffalo milled in frightened circles, or galloped
heavily from the fringes of the frantic herd. White men and
red, guiding nimble ponies with their knees, spun, charged
and leaped through the surging mass of bulls, cows and calves.
Hunters swung their muskets low, fired and whirled away
from the huge beasts somersaulting in death. Then, still at
full gallop, the riders would plunge hands into pockets, scoop
up loose powder, pour it into hot gun barrels, spit lead balls

from their mouths, and look around for the next victims. Muskets roared; buffalo bellowed. Perhaps in the appalling confusion of the hunt, a pony might slip, the thin body of an Indian turn darkly against the sky and plunge shrieking into the grinding mass of buffalo hoofs.

An hour later the herd would be gone, but a hundred dead buffalo and the torn body of an Indian boy would remain on the grass of the prairie.

Strange as it may seem, a big beast called the buffalo, or bison, shaped the course of history in western Canada and the United States of America. To begin with, it is believed that the buffalo played a part in forming the prairies that swept from the Great Lakes to the Rockies and downward into the Mississippi Valley. No trees could survive where the great herds held sway. Scratching their tough hides on the bark, they soon wore away the protective covering and the trees died.

No other large animal has ever existed in such tremendous numbers, nor has any been so well suited to cope with the difficulties of life. A buffalo bull was as tall as a man, as long as an automobile and heavier than a small truck. His temper was hot and his strength fantastic. The big herds lived through severe weather that killed horses and cattle—facing blizzards and howling winds, pawing the snows to eat the frozen grasses. Even the new-born calves, lying in the drifts, soon struggled to their feet and hobbled to the shelter of their mothers' bodies. Although the buffalo cow had only one calf at a time, she continued to bear young season after season, often for thirty years. So down through the centuries the herds grew larger and larger until millions of them roamed the continent from the barren lands to the Gulf of Mexico.

Long before the French and Spanish came to the West, the Indians were hunting and killing the beast that nature had provided so generously. To the red men the buffalo was

The buffalo hunt was marked by scenes of wild confusion as great herds of huge beasts stampeded before the guns and horses of Indians and white men.

home, food and life itself: from the meat they had food; from the hides tepees and clothing; from the sinews thread and string; from the horns spoons, headdresses and ornaments. Sinews became bow cords, and the lining of the buffalo's stomach became water bottles. Living off the big animal as they did, the plains Indians were strong and healthy, while the swift movements of the hunt gave them agility and courage. Under these conditions it is not surprising that the braves of the plains were such skilled and daring warriors.

The fresh meat from the hunt was not the only form in which buffalo flesh was eaten, since the natives were experts in the making of *pemmican*. This was made from dried buffalo meat, pounded to a powder, mixed with fat and stored in leather bags. While not delicious in taste, it was a nourishing food and very convenient for carrying on long trips by horse, canoe or even on foot. The roaming fur trader lived on pemmican, and such large trading firms as the Hudson's Bay Company and the North-West Company stocked supplies of it for the use of the factors, voyageurs and explorers. No other single item of provision was as important to the restless white men who paddled the western streams or followed the buffalo trails to the rim of the prairies.

Years later, the railways came to the plains and brought final doom to the majestic herds, a doom that came with startling speed. Armies of railway workers were fed on buffalo steaks and tongues supplied by professional hunters, and, as the trains began moving westward, passengers amused themselves by shooting the animals from the windows of the moving cars. Bodies were left to rot in the hot sun of the prairies, and bleached bones strewed the brown dry grasses.

Both red men and white joined in the senseless slaughter. The great bulk of the buffalo herds disappeared in the 1870's and by 1885, only a handful of the mighty animals remained in all the West. Indian tribes which had once lived in plenty, were reduced to poverty and starvation. Fortunately the Canadian government took measures to protect the few remaining buffalo, and today the well-kept herds number some fifteen thousand.

The buffalo was saved from complete destruction, but the magnificent millions known to the early Indians have gone the way of the passenger pigeon.

16   SAMUEL HEARNE

During the year 1768 the traders of the Hudson's Bay Company post at Churchill were thrown into a state of excitement by some samples of ore brought to the post by northern Indians.

"By thunder," roared Moses Norton, "that's copper, and mighty good ore it is too!"

Factor Norton was not a man to stand around doing nothing while mineral fortunes lay in wait, so he took the next boat to England and asked permission of the directors of the Company to send an expedition to the barren lands in search of copper.

Permission was readily granted and a young man, Samuel Hearne, was named as leader. This Hearne was a remarkable person. At eleven years of age he had joined the British Royal Navy and had seen battle action during the first months of his service. After leaving the navy, he joined the Hudson's Bay Company, came to Canada, and took a post as mate on a company ship trading in Hudson Bay. Hearne was still but twenty-four years of age when he was made leader of the copper expedition to the north.

The young sailor was chosen for exploration because he

had wide knowledge in navigation, astronomy, surveying and map-making. Such skills were necessary so that careful records could be kept of the exact routes travelled by the party. His orders from the Company were very full, and it became clear to him that he was expected to do a great deal more than merely find copper. He was to travel to the Athabaska district, search for a stream known as the Copper Mine River and follow it to the sea. He was to talk with Indian tribes and learn the possibilities of fur trade, and lastly he was to watch for any waterways that might lead to a Western Sea.

The expedition starting from Fort Prince of Wales at Churchill in November, 1769, was made up of Hearne, two other white men and a small group of Indians. As they moved away from the post cannon boomed a salute of farewell from the stone walls of the fortress. It soon became apparent to Hearne that his Indians were by no means trustworthy and that they planned to cause trouble. For two hundred miles he made his way across the barren lands, suffering from cold and hunger, only to have the Indians desert the expedition. In five weeks' time Hearne made a sheepish return to the fort on Hudson Bay, confessing that the journey had been a dismal failure.

Undiscouraged by this first attempt, three months later Hearne set off in the snow with three Indians as travelling mates. Northward into the dismal barren lands they marched, through the winter and into the spring months. The snow melted, they gave up their snowshoes, and plodded on, each man with a pack on his back. They were well north of the forests, and wood was so scarce that they could not erect their little tent or light fires to cook game and fish. They ate raw meat. Then fish and animals disappeared, so that for a time they were reduced to living on old leather, burned bones and a few wild berries, a poor diet for men walking twenty

Samuel Hearne with Chief Matonabbee and a group of Indians travelled across the Barren Lands of northern Canada in search of the Coppermine River. Even during the winter months they could march eighteen miles a day.

miles a day. They were saved from starvation when they joined a band of wandering Indian hunters who found caribou and other game in plenty. Hearne's guides, satisfied with this bountiful life, refused to travel farther north with the explorer.

During August Hearne's quadrant was broken by accident, and he no longer was able to record his movements accurately. It was useless to go on, so he turned once again toward Churchill. It is possible that he and the Indians would have starved to death on the lonely wastes had it not been for a chance meeting with an Indian chief called Matonabbee. This generous red man, finding the wanderers hungry and exhausted, gave them buckskin clothing and food from his own supplies. Then as a final gesture of good will, he accompanied Hearne back to Hudson Bay. During the course of the journey, the young explorer took a great liking to the chief and a strong friendship grew between them.

It was good to be back to the warmth and comfort of the post, but Hearne after a few days became restless. In less than two weeks' time he was off again into the barrens accompanied by his friend Matonabbee. Instead of striking northward as on the two other trips, the party moved westward along the southern rim of the barren lands in the direction of Great Slave Lake. They had dogs and sleighs, but these could not carry all the supplies and Hearne's instruments: each man carried a heavy pack. At the rate of about eighteen miles a day they fought through heavy snow and cutting winds. After a dull, miserable Christmas they came to a forest where some of Matonabbee's people were camped. Here, to Hearne's surprise, the chief added some squaws to the party, explaining with a smile that no expedition in the north could be successful without Indian women. The squaws, he said, could do as much work as two men, they could make clothes and moccasins, they could pull sleighs, cook and put up tepees. The chief himself had no less than eight wives.

They resumed their march toward the West, enjoying fine hunting among the caribou herds and stopping from time to time to have big feasts on juicy steaks. Spring came, and by May they were at Clowey Lake where they built canoes from bark and wood carried from the woods. A large band of Indians at the lake asked if they might go along with the explorers and Hearne agreed to this plan. The waters were still frozen over, but they marched northward carrying the canoes on their shoulders. Matonabbee assured Hearne that he knew the way to the Coppermine River, so the young explorer put full faith in his friend's wide wisdom concerning the barren lands.

As they moved northward, women, children and dogs were left behind in a camp so that the men might push forward with greater speed. Many of the Indians, becoming tired of travel, dropped away, but Hearne, Matonabbee and about one hundred and fifty braves went on.

After carrying the canoes for a month, ice broke up in the waterways and they were able to use the craft for the first time in crossing a river with a remarkable name—Congecatha-wachaga. Here they came to a camp of Copper Indians who had never seen a white man before. They looked Hearne over curiously, remarked on the peculiar colour of his skin and his hair, which they said was like a buffalo's tail.

As they moved on, some of the Copper Indians went along, swelling the numbers of the party. About the middle of July they reached the Coppermine River which foamed about huge dark boulders set firmly in the bed of the stream. It was a wild and primitive scene, marked by bare rocks and short twisted trees that writhed against the sky.

Soon after they reached the river, advance scouts discovered a small camp of Eskimos—five tents set out on a flat rock near a waterfall. Hurrying back to the main party, the scouts reported the camp and threw the Indians into a state of frenzy. Chattering excitedly, they ran for their shields and weapons, jumping and whooping in delight. To Hearne's horror he realized that his travelling companions were making ready to attack the Eskimo camp. Nothing he could say would have any effect on the bloodthirsty red men busy painting their shields with the symbols of earth and air. In a long wavering line the Indians snaked along the river bank, keeping low among the rocks. When they came in sight of the camp, they took off their heavier clothing, tied back their hair and daubed their faces with red and black.

Then, circling the sleeping camp from the land side, they charged with whoops that echoed across the barrens. Half-dressed Eskimos in a dazed state tumbled from their beds and rushed outdoors to stare dumbly at the horde of painted Indians. There was no escape save the rushing river, and they did not try that. Helplessly, Hearne watched as every man, woman and child in the camp was massacred on the grey rock.

Tents, poles, food and Eskimo weapons were ripped apart and hurled into the roaring waterfall.

Strange as it may seem fifty years later the great polar explorer, Sir John Franklin, visited that spot and found the bones and skulls of the poor Eskimos still lying on the river's edge.

A few days after the Eskimo camp was wiped out, the party reached the mouth of the Coppermine and looked across a narrow stretch of open water to a great ice pack that lay like a gigantic white plain. Hearne had reached the Arctic Ocean! After making a small cairn by piling up a mound of loose stones, he claimed the land in the name of the Hudson's Bay Company.

Hearne was at the mouth of the Coppermine River, but where was the copper? Discouraged, he turned southward along the river, but on the second day of the trip homeward, the Indians led him to a spot some thirty miles inland from the sea. Here, in a weird place of jumbled rocks, the Indians said were great quantities of the mineral. Searching quickly

The Indians took off their heavier clothing, and tied back their hair. Then, clutching their weapons, they crept silently toward the sleeping Eskimo camp.

Hearne found some samples of ore, but felt that no great wealth in copper existed in that region. Carrying a four-pound piece of metal he left the place and turned back to the river.

During the following twelve months Hearne made his way southward to Great Slave Lake and then eastward across the barrens to Fort Prince of Wales. He had been gone one year, six months and twenty-three days.

Hearne continued in the service of the Hudson's Bay Company, became governor of Fort Prince of Wales, and later died in England after retiring from the fur trade.

HEARNE EXPLORATIONS

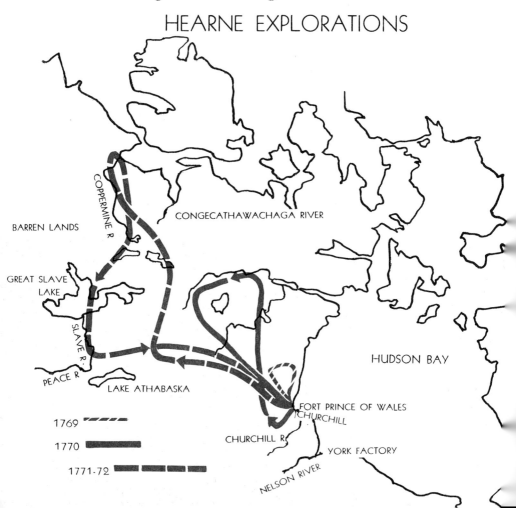

Samuel Hearne has not received full honours due him in history. His explorations were so wide and difficult that they have never been repeated. His notes on bird and animal life were made so carefully that even famous scientists admire them. His charts were so accurate that they formed a basis for future maps. His writings were so charming they thrilled thousands of readers. Perhaps strangest of all is the fact that he tamed wild beaver on Hudson Bay a century and a half before the days of Grey Owl.

17   ALEXANDER HENRY

In 1759 General James Wolfe captured Quebec and Canada became British. This brought rapid changes in the trading business, for Englishmen and Scots moved westward into the fur lands that had been controlled by the French.

A genial French trader of Montreal smiled at the young Englishman. "Monsieur Henry," he said, "this is no place to make money. To gain a big fortune you must go to the prairie country far to the west of the Great Lakes. Ah, what furs come out of that country! I have seen them myself, canoe after canoe of them—fox, beaver, marten and muskrat. Those pelts make my eyes shine and my fingers itch. My friend, if I were a sturdy *garçon* like you, I would get a canoe and head for the West!"

Alexander Henry rubbed his cheek and looked thoughtful. "It sounds so easy," he laughed. "I get into a canoe, go West and presto—I'm a wealthy man!"

The trader shrugged his shoulders. "But no, it will not be easy. I did not say that! Those Indians in the West still like us French, and they hate you English. Blood will be spilled . . . but a good English trader could go to the prairies, make his peace with the Indians, and come out with plenty of furs."

Alexander Henry clapped the Frenchman on the shoulder. "I'll do it!" he shouted. "Thanks to you for your advice."

True to his word, the following year Henry, then just twenty-two years of age, set off from Lachine with a supply of trading goods and started the long journey to the West. Like Du Lhut, he went up the Ottawa, crossed to Lake Huron, and on to Mackinac.

As the French trader in Montreal had stated so frankly, the Indians of the West still remained loyal to the French, and held a deep resentment toward the British conquerors of Canada. A clever and skilful chieftain, Pontiac, had rallied many of the tribes and was stirring them up to drive the British from their newly-won lands.

While Alexander Henry was still at Mackinac, Pontiac's warriors carried out a treacherous attack against that trading centre. The red men, pretending to be very friendly toward the British, invited them to watch a lacrosse match in front of the fort. While the game was in progress, warriors rushed through the gate of the stockade, attacked the garrison and killed many of the soldiers in the first onslaught. The rest fell one by one. Henry, hearing the noise of the attack, ran to the attic of a French trader's house and hid himself hastily under a pile of birch bark. The following day he was captured, and nearly lost his life when a big brave, wielding a knife, chased him round and round in circles. Indians laughed at these antics, but it was not so funny to Henry. By quick footwork he escaped death on this occasion, and later won his freedom through the good will of an Indian who adopted him as a brother.

After spending two more years in the Lake Superior district, Henry started on a journey to the far West by way of Rainy River, Lake of the Woods, and Winnipeg River to Lake Winnipeg. There he met other British traders: Peter Pond and the two Frobisher brothers. Travelling on together, they

Alexander Henry left the Lake Superior country, and started out for the fur lands of the far west. During the long journey he made many portages from one waterway to another. Here we see him carrying a birch bark canoe.

arrived at the Saskatchewan River and after a hard paddle upstream came to Cumberland House, a post which had been established the year before by Samuel Hearne of the Hudson's Bay Company. Despite the fact that the visitors were trading rivals, the factor gave them a warm welcome and extended the hospitality of the post.

The following year Alexander Henry decided to advance farther west to hunt and explore the country, and as he went he paddled up the Saskatchewan to Fort des Prairies. There he joined a band of Assiniboines who were snowshoeing to the place of their winter camp. So rapidly did the red men travel, that Henry was hard put to maintain the pace. The snow was deep, and the trail was broken by the squaws and dogs which drew packs on wooden travois. At night they cleared away the snow for a camp, set up a few tepees and feasted on buffalo tongues that were put to boil in Henry's iron kettle. It was a long, arduous trip for the Englishman, but nevertheless he enjoyed the keen cold air, the breathtaking sweep of the prairies and the sight of buffalo herds they passed from time to time.

In the spring of 1775 Henry joined the Frobisher brothers at a new post which they had erected on the Churchill River some distance north of Cumberland House. The traders explored the Churchill and came in contact with the Chippewayan Indians who told Henry of a chain of lakes and rivers lying to the west—Peace, Slave, Athabaska. The tribesmen led Henry to believe that the ocean was but a short distance north of Slave Lake. The Chippewayans did not realize that salt water was many days travel north of the lakes and rivers they mentioned, a fact which was later proved by Alexander Mackenzie.

After travelling and trading for over fifteen years, Henry returned to Montreal, became a merchant, and made a fortune for himself. He became famous for other reasons than trade and travel, however, for he wrote a book concerning his western wanderings, *Travels and Adventures in Canada and the Indian Territories between the Years 1760 and 1776*. Henry could not have possessed much education, and yet he produced this charming book which is an outstanding piece of descriptive writing.

He sailed to England and there he made friends with a number of very important people who took great pleasure in his company. Even more interesting than this, however, is the fact that he crossed to France, was received by the King, and while in the palace, he entertained Queen Marie Antoinette with tales of his western wanderings. It was a memorable scene—the white haired trader talking excitedly to the famous beauty of the French court.

The English adventurer who had dared to invade the Indian lands alone died in Montreal, 1824, when he was eighty-five years of age.

18 THE NOR' WESTERS

Traders such as Alexander Henry, Peter Pond and the Frobisher brothers came to be known as the Nor' Westers. They were men who worked out of Montreal either singly or in small bands, and as the years went by they increased in numbers, spreading their trade across the lands of the west and northwest. Among these hardy traders were Englishmen, French-Canadians and Yankees, but most of them were stern Scots from the Highlands.

As soon as the ice cleared from the St. Lawrence in early spring, Montreal became a hustling, bustling place as the traders and voyageurs jumped to the task of loading their forty-foot freight canoes. Into these huge birch bark boats could be packed four tons of trading goods together with a dozen voyageurs.

After saying a last prayer at the little chapel of Ste. Anne, the paddlers pushed up the Ottawa, travelling most of the daylight hours. The tough, gay voyageurs, feathers stuck in their jaunty caps, sang French songs to the swing of the glistening paddles. In the evening they tied up to the river bank and went ashore among the trees. Black iron pots were slung over the flames, camp fires glowed in the warm dusk,

After the day's paddling, the traders and voyageurs camped on shore. They sat about open fires, eating, smoking their pipes, singing and telling stories.

and the odour of pea soup, pork and pemmican tickled the noses of the hungry men.

On they went to the upper reaches of the Ottawa, across Lake Huron, through the St. Mary's River, over Lake Superior to *Grand Portage*, the great meeting place of the fur brigades. It was here that the light canoes of the western fur lands met the heavy freight canoes from Montreal during the months of June and July. *Grand Portage* was the most colourful, lively and exciting place in the whole history of the fur trade. Beaded Indians, tanned voyageurs, Scottish traders and eastern merchants mingled together in the amazing business of the fur trade. Old friends met joyfully after years of absence, traders hired voyageurs, contracts were signed, furs examined, stories told, and loud celebrations turned into drunken brawls.

There was the swift transfer of cargoes: provisions and trade goods going into the light western canoes, the packs of furs being stowed away aboard the big Montreal freighters. Then in a few days' time the brigades separated, furs moving eastward, trade goods westward to the fur lands. *Grand Portage* was left far behind.

The little canoes headed westward on the old route of Pierre La Vérendrye—Rainy River, Rainy Lake, Lake of the Woods, Lake Winnipeg and on to the distant trading posts. It was often necessary to portage the canoes over land lying between rivers and lakes or about seething rapids. The little French-Canadian voyageurs were masters of this art, trotting easily over rocky trails with canoes and bulky loads. Packs were all made up in ninety-pound bundles, and a good voyageur could carry two or more of these on his bent back. It was the wiry, good-humoured French-Canadian voyageurs who made the long canoe routes possible.

The Hudson's Bay Company, according to its charter, held all rights to the western fur trade. The Nor' Westers knew this, of course, but they paid it little attention as they pushed westward and northward across the plains and forests, building posts on the rivers and lakes. Becoming alarmed by the swift actions of the Montreal traders, the Hudson's Bay Company decided that its posts, too, must be planted in the West. In 1774, the great explorer, Samuel Hearne, was sent to the Saskatchewan River and there he built the Company's first inland post, Fort Cumberland.

In the beginning, the Nor' Westers worked alone or in small groups, competing against each other for the fur wealth of the West. They were shrewd, hard business men who did not hesitate to take advantage of each other, and their trading methods were not always honest. Rum and whiskey were exchanged for furs, causing hardship, suffering and sudden death. Indian braves, mad with liquor, went into frenzied rages, running amok in the camps, killing and maiming their fellow red men. A number of Nor' Westers, too, lost their lives in drunken squabbles.

Just at a time when it appeared that the Indians might rise against the traders, the dread disease of smallpox swept across the fur lands, and the Indians perished by the hundreds.

The Nor' Westers had learned their lesson. They knew that if they were to survive and hold their own against the Hudson's Bay Company, they must join forces among themselves. Accordingly, in 1784, the great North West Company was formed in Montreal.

Then the two powerful rivals, the North West Company and the Hudson's Bay Company, faced each other in a bitter struggle for the fur trade, which sent traders scurrying across mountains, down rivers and through forests, to the farthest corners of the Canadian wilderness. Canoe brigades dotted the shining waters, voyageurs sang their songs, dog teams panted across the plains, and hungry explorers snowshoed over the barren lands as the struggle for more and still more furs progressed.

NORTHWEST AND NORTH

19   VITUS BERING

Much of North America had been claimed by the Spanish, French and English before Russia began any exploration in the New World. Then in 1725, Czar Peter the Great, anxious to make Russia a great world power, sent an expedition to the Pacific under a Danish seaman, Vitus Bering. Bering sailed north and reached what we now call Bering Straits. Here is the story of his second great journey which took place after the death of the Czar.

Vitus Bering reined up his tough little saddle pony and looked back on the swaying procession that snaked its way across the dusty plains of Russia. On they came, hundreds of them—Cossack cavalrymen, monks, physicians, artists, botanists, geographers, historians, boatmen, servants, labourers —riding and walking in the dusty confusion of shuffling pack horses.

Bering let the reins fall on his pony's neck and a faint smile broke across his face. "I'll show these Russians!" he said. "The stupid scholars scoff at my tales of seeing the unknown waterway that lies between Asia and America. They point to their silly maps and whine that it cannot be, since a continent called Gamaland stands somewhere between Siberia and the New World. Such nonsense! I'll show them what I have done and what I have seen. I'll march them six thousand miles across Russia and I'll sail them through Pacific waters to prove that Gamaland is a child's dream!"

He picked up the reins, prodded the pony with his heels and turned back into the plodding procession.

Here was one of the strangest expeditions in all the history of exploration, an army of soldiers, scholars and slaves struggling across mountains, tundras, swamps, dry plains and flooded rivers; struggling on to the Pacific. Mad Peter the Great, Czar of Russia, had dreamed before his death of Russia reaching out to the New World for land and riches as other nations had done; and now, ten years after his death, Vitus Bering was making his second expedition to the Pacific.

The hardy Dane led his cumbersome company eastward, month after month, year after year, stopping from time to time at Russian forts to rest and secure more supplies. Men died, horses dropped from exhaustion, the scholars complained, and soldiers deserted to the roving bands of bandits. They crossed swift rivers in wide rafts, climbed mountain trails, trudged across dreary barren lands, shivered and stumbled through snow storms. Three winters they spent in the frigid mountains of Siberia.

Finally they reached the Peninsula of Kamchatka on the shores of the Pacific just to the south of Bering Sea, and there they set up headquarters, complete with houses, a church, a fort and barracks for the soldiers. Boatbuilders brought along for the purpose, started work on the construction of two sailing ships, and in the course of time they finished the *St. Peter* and the *St. Paul*.

By June, 1741, Bering was ready to begin his oceanic explorations. The bell in the church tolled and the cannon fired from the walls of the fort as the two ships drew away from shore and headed out onto the Pacific.

The scholars that Bering carried with him insisted that

Bering's two ships sailed from Russia into the Atlantic searching for a mysterious continent called "Gamaland." As they sailed on, wind, fog and snow swept out of the night. The two vessels were separated in the wild storm. Did they find Gamaland?

Gamaland would be found by sailing in a southward direction toward the shores of America. Bering, they said, had missed Gamaland on his first voyage because he had sailed too far north. The Dane knew that no such land existed, but he could do nothing against the determination of the stubborn scholars. Winds, fog and snow swept down from the north, buffeting the ships and separating them in the confusion of the storm. Great waves curled over the sides of the vessels and sent water gurgling across the decks. When the fog and the storm had passed away, the seamen and the scholars on board the *St. Peter* could find no trace of either the *St. Paul* or of Gamaland. Bering hid a smile at the bewilderment of the scholars, who had become sullen and angry with disappointment. For a month they searched for the missing *St. Paul,* and having no luck, the ship turned northward.

Conditions by this time were becoming serious on board the *St. Peter.* The weather was hot, food supplies were running low, drinking water was stale, and Bering fell ill with scurvy.

The ship moved northward through thick fogs well out from the coast of America, passing along the shores of what is now British Columbia. As the skies cleared, the crew saw driftwood floating on the water and seabirds flying overhead. It was evident that they were not far from land. Then one morning there was a loud shout, a scramble of feet on the deck and an excited pointing of hands to the east. Men from below rushed on deck and ran to the rails to join the eager watchers. Bering, pale and weak, appeared in his night clothes to look on a rocky Alaskan beach, the blue wall of a glacier, a high mountain peak, and a meadow spotted with wild flowers and grasses that sloped down to the waters.

Seamen and scholars shouted like Indians, hugged each other and danced wildly on the decks. Bering remained silent, all wrapped in gloomy thoughts. "Let them dance," he thought. "They know nothing of our position, nor how we will ever get back to Kamchatka!"

After a short stay, Bering ordered the ship to sail against the protests of the scholars, who wished to remain and explore. But the sick Dane knew that with a battered ship and a low food supply they might never make the long voyage back to Russia.

Time proved that Bering was right. The *St. Peter* threaded
her way among the Aleutian Islands, dodging shoals and
shallows in the baffling light of heavy fogs. Then one night the
faltering vessel wandered too close to land and was drawn
shoreward by a strong current which pushed the vessel
aground. Next morning the rip tide raised the *St. Peter* and
she resumed the horrible voyage.

Provisions were now so low that the men were chewing on
rotten sea biscuits and drinking stale water. Scholars whined,
argued and fought with each other, or prayed to Heaven for
deliverance from starvation and shipwreck. By November new
land appeared ahead, and at first glance the anxious crew
believed it to be Kamchatka, but their screams of delight died
away when they found it was but another of the endless islands
they had been skirting for weeks past.

Actually they were within a few days sailing time of their
home port. Bering urged that they sail on, but the frightened
men demanded that the ship be sailed into the dismal cove on
the barren shore. Too weak to stand, Bering was helped ashore
by the seamen. He shook his head sadly as he looked over the
island—there was food in the form of sea-cows, foxes and seals,
but no trees to build huts for protection during the coming
winter.

They dug pits in the ground, lined the walls with peat and
roofed them over with sea moss . . . poor protection from the
howling winds of Siberia. Shivering from cold, gulping bits of
raw meat, they lived miserably in their black holes. A hurricane
struck the *St. Peter,* snapped her anchor rope and hurled the
ship on the beach, a shattered mass of timbers.

As a bitter wind screamed about his shelter on a morning
in December, Vitus Bering mumbled a few prayers and died,
wrapped in his dirty fur robes. His last thoughts were ones of
disappointment and hopelessness.

In the spring of 1742, a few desperate survivors of the

expedition crawled from their gloomy pits on Bering Island and made plans to escape from the desolate shores. They killed hundreds of strange sea animals that swarmed the shallow waters after storms, and from the glossy furs fashioned clumsy pieces of clothing. Laboriously they constructed a raft from the timbers of the *St. Peter*, fitted it with a patched sail and banks of oars. In this awkward craft they set out in search of Kamchatka, and by a miracle they reached port in safety. Fantastic figures they appeared, with their long hair and beards, their half-naked bodies draped in tattered garments of fur.

Among the astonished people who saw them come ashore at Kamchatka was a small group of Chinese merchants who took great interest in the furs of the wild-looking men on the raft. The Chinese examined the furs eagerly and paid gold for all the survivors possessed.

This was the beginning of the great sea-otter trade which sent hundreds of Russian traders roaming through the Aleutian Islands and on to the shores of Alaska in search of the water animals with the beautiful fur. Here was a trade which was later to excite the British and the Spanish, but, in the end, led to near extinction of the glossy animal that swam the Pacific waters.

20 ALEXANDER MACKENZIE

As the posts of the North West Company and the Hudson's Bay Company spread across the plains and forests, the traders pushed farther west and farther north, seeking new lands for the fur trade. The achievements of these dauntless explorers represent a sparkling chapter in the history of the Americas.

I

In the gloomy interior of a trading post on Lake Athabaska a slim Scotsman, Alexander Mackenzie, was grading furs, running his fingers over the soft pelts. He turned toward his cousin who was working nearby and spoke quietly. "Roderick," he asked, "do ye think it's good fur country north of here?"

Roderick Mackenzie looked at Alexander curiously. "I dinna ken," he replied, "but I am thinking that ye have something in mind."

The fur trader smiled. "If we Nor' Westers expect to take trade away from the Hudson's Bay Company we'll have to explore more land and open more posts. I'm going to take a few men and make a wee trip along the Slave to see what's in the north country. Who can tell—I may even reach the ocean!"

Roderick's face crinkled into a broad grin. "I thought ye

had something under your bonnet! Ye've been as restless as an old she-bear! I believe ye'd rather travel than trade any day."

"Aye," said Alexander, "that I would!"

On June 3, 1789, Mackenzie left the North West Company post on Lake Athabaska with four canoes manned by voyageurs and Indians. They pushed across the lake, entered the Slave River, and after six days paddling, came to Great Slave Lake in strong winds, rain and high waves. Mackenzie knew that another stream led northward from the big lake, but finding it proved difficult. Even with the help of local Indians from the Yellow Knife tribe, it was the end of June before they discovered the river they were seeking.

On the first day of July the canoes entered the new river and nosed down stream, gliding easily in the deep, smooth current. It was a glorious time for travel, as the northern sun shone for twenty hours a day, and the big river offered no obstacles. At Great Bear Lake they met strange, shy Indians who had to be coaxed into talking with the explorers. These tribesmen, when their friendship was won, begged Mackenzie not to go farther down river, because of waterfalls and great monsters that lay ahead.

Not the least bit alarmed by the Indian tales, Mackenzie and his party paddled down stream, finding nothing more dangerous than thick clouds of mosquitoes that hummed and buzzed about their heads. Further north they picked up an Indian guide who told them that they were not far from the ocean, and this news heartened the men of the group. As they went on, the trees grew smaller and smaller, islands in the river became barren flats, the guide grew frightened and urged Mackenzie to turn back. Even the voyageurs were alarmed, and Mackenzie was forced to promise his men that if the ocean was not reached within a week's time, they would turn back.

The hours of sunlight grew longer and longer until there was no darkness at all . . . trees had almost disappeared . . . the dark shores were cold and forbidding . . . signs of Eskimo camps were seen here and there . . . showers and keen winds chilled the paddlers . . . they looked sullen and frightened.

The river divided into wide channels of shallow water that wriggled between the islands like fat snakes. On July 12, Mackenzie and one of the men climbed a hill and looked across the grim countryside.

"Look!" shouted Mackenzie, waving his arm toward a field of ice that spread away to the northwest.

"The sea!" gasped his companion.

That night their camp was nearly washed away by the rush of the ocean tide thrusting down the river channel.

The party, once more in good humour, thrilled to the sight of green Arctic waters, dark between the ice floes. They shouted in excitement at the sight of some whales, and hurried into a canoe to give chase to the black monsters. By good fortune a grey polar fog settled down over the scene and put an end to the foolhardy hunt.

For three days they stayed on the Arctic shores and then they started back up the stream now called the Mackenzie River. It was a rapid, quiet journey which took two months of paddling time; they arrived at the post on Lake Athabaska after an absence of one hundred and two days.

Knowing as we do the present mineral wealth of the northwest, it is most interesting to read that Mackenzie reported seeing oil and coal during the course of this journey.

II

Having conquered the northern river and reached the Arctic Ocean, Mackenzie looked about for other regions to explore. His interest reached a peak when he heard stories of

Russian and Spanish seamen who were making fortunes in the sea-otter trade on the Pacific coast of America. A glossy, dark animal, the sea-otter, was easily caught by the coastal Indians and traded to seamen for cheap articles of metal.

Excited by the prospects of a coastal fur trade, Mackenzie's active mind formed dreams of crossing through the mountains and reaching the ocean. In order to prepare for such an expedition, he spent a winter in London, England, studying astronomy and surveying, and by spring of 1793 he was back on the Athabaska ready to make the westward dash to the Pacific. A giant canoe, twenty-five feet long and capable of carrying a ton and a half of cargo, had been especially built for the journey. Into this sturdy craft, loaded with provisions, stepped Mackenzie, another trader, six voyageurs and two Indian guides. It was May 9, 1793.

They headed westward into the fast current of the Peace River, paddling hard against the push of the water or poling slowly over sparkling shallows. A week later the river narrowed into a dark gorge where the current tore through sheer walls of rock with a force that made paddling impossible. Mackenzie shook his head as he watched the foaming water race by the canoe.

After a short hesitation, he secured a long rope, tied it to the thwart of the canoe, took the other end, leaped to the steep slope of the bank and began the slow climb upward, cutting footholds as he went. He clung tightly to the rocky wall, as the river roared below and his men watched tensely. At last he reached the top and signalled his men to follow. Painfully they dragged the canoe and packs of provisions up the slope and made ready for the long tough portage around the rapids, nine miles in length.

They struggled on day after day, carrying the canoe and packs of food, and at night they dropped exhausted into their blankets. Finally they came to the end of the rapids, put the

In dugout canoes borrowed from the Indians, Mackenzie and his men paddled down the Bella Coola River to the Pacific Ocean. Compare these wooden canoes with the one pictured on page 71. Dugout canoes were carved from a single log by the Indians of the west coast.

canoe in the water, and paddled on, coming days later to the Parsnip River, a branch of the Peace, which turned sharply to the south. As they moved upstream, they could hear the thunderous grumble of landslides among the mountain peaks. At the source of the Parsnip they portaged over a ridge and set the canoe in the headwaters of the Fraser River which flowed southward through the mountains.

Here for the first time they were travelling with the river current, not against it, and it was a wonderful feeling for the paddlers. Their relief, however, was short-lived, for the canoe was thrust forward so swiftly they could not control its motion. Riding sideways, the craft bucked down the rapids with the men hanging desperately to the thwarts, terrorized by the heaving water and the speed of their flight. With a splintering crash the canoe rammed a sandbar, ripping off the stern and dousing the packs with foam. By heroic efforts the men dragged the broken craft ashore, spread out the provisions to dry, and set to work on repairs.

Continuing down stream, they had little more adventure until they met some whooping Carrier Indians who shot arrows and rolled boulders into the river. Mackenzie ordered his men to land on the opposite shore, and then he proceeded to make friends with the tribesmen. After receiving a few gifts, the red men warmed up to the explorers and even offered some good advice on how to reach the ocean. The party, they said, should follow a branch of the Fraser called the Blackwater rather than follow the main course of the big stream.

Mackenzie decided to follow this suggestion, and with a Carrier guide aboard the canoe, they paddled up the Blackwater to its source. There they left the canoe, cached some food, and set off through the forest with heavy packs on their backs. It was hard, tough travel through the dim, wet woods, over a faint trail that wound over ridges and down into deep valleys. Their shoes wore out and their clothes hung in rags, but they plodded on to the Bella Coola River where generous Indians loaned them several dugout canoes. Once again afloat, they paddled down the short stream, eagerly watching for the first signs of the coast. The sturdy dugouts passed long fish traps set out by the Indians and soon afterwards the men sniffed the unmistakable tang of the sea. On Saturday, July 20, 1793, they came to the river's mouth and stared happily at the face of the Pacific.

Two days later, Mackenzie stood in his tattered clothes, a smile on his face, as he wrote in red paint on the side of a rock:

> *Alexander Mackenzie, from Canada, by land, the twenty-second of July, one thousand seven hundred and ninety-three. Lat. 52° 20′ 48″ N.*

MACKENZIE, FRASER, THOMPSON

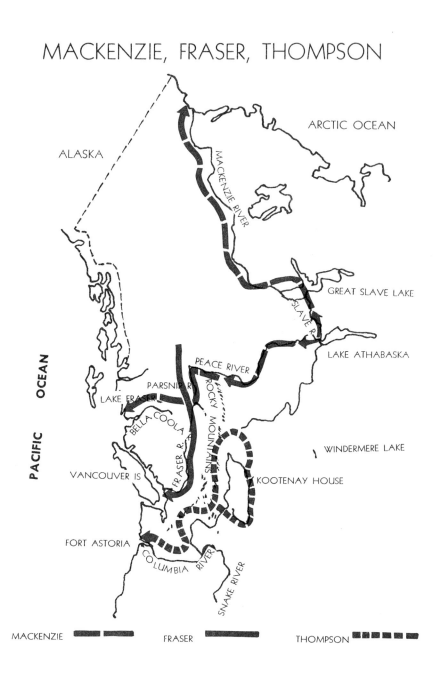

ARCTIC OCEAN

ALASKA

MACKENZIE RIVER

GREAT SLAVE LAKE

SLAVE R.

LAKE ATHABASKA

PEACE RIVER

PARSNIP R.

LAKE FRASER

BELLA COOLA

ROCKY MOUNTAINS

WINDERMERE LAKE

OCEAN

PACIFIC

VANCOUVER IS

FRASER R.

KOOTENAY HOUSE

FORT ASTORIA

COLUMBIA RIVER

SNAKE RIVER

MACKENZIE ▬▬ ▬ ▬   FRASER ▬▬▬▬   THOMPSON ▪▪▪▪▪▪

In the long race for the Pacific by land which had begun in the days of Cartier, Champlain and La Salle, Mackenzie had won, and his restless spirit was well content with the outcome. Not long after this historic journey he left Canada and returned to Scotland where he wrote the story of his travels. In 1802, he became Sir Alexander Mackenzie when he was knighted by the King for his great work.

21   SIMON FRASER

For some years after Mackenzie's overland journey the Nor'
Westers took little interest in the Pacific, but the time came when
they had to take action. Russians were sailing Alaskan waters and
American traders had their eyes on the coastal fur lands. In 1808
another explorer of the North West Company took to his canoe and
headed for the rugged coast.

It was a lazy day in 1806. Carrier Indians on the shores
of Lake Stuart moved about their camp or sat in the shade of
tall trees that swayed softly in a light breeze. A young lad
playing on the beach stopped running, shaded his eyes and
gazed across the waters.

"White men!" he shouted. The tribesmen gathered quickly
along the shore and watched in astonishment as two enormous
canoes skipped across the lake in the direction of the camp.
The swift beat of the voyageurs' paddles sent the long craft
galloping over the low waves.

The paddlers swept into land, traders jumped ashore and
pointing their muskets to the sky, fired a volley of celebration.
Then the leader of the party, Simon Fraser, turned to the
Carrier Indians, smiled in a friendly manner, and set his men

to passing out gifts among the Indians—tobacco for the braves and soap for the squaws. The red men looked at the tobacco curiously, not knowing what to do with it; the squaws sniffed at the soap and, thinking it was good to eat, commenced to chew on it. Before the traders could stop them they were making terrible faces and were frothing at their mouths. Laughing aloud, Fraser had to explain that the women's gifts were for washing and not for eating.

The newcomers found themselves in one of the most beautiful regions that they had ever seen. Lake Stuart, studded by green islands, twisted back and forth for a distance of fifty miles. The slopes of the Rocky Mountains covered with rippling forests rose from the smooth waters to above scattered clouds that hung white and soft like clean wool. So pleased was Fraser with the region that he gave it the name New Caledonia, meaning "New Scotland," the first name for British Columbia.

A clearing was made in the forest and in a few weeks' time a new trading post of the North West Company stood in the centre of a strong palisade. Trading with the Carriers began at once, and soon bales of furs were piling up in the storeroom of the post.

Simon Fraser, like Alexander Mackenzie, had more interest in exploration than he had in the fur business, so he was not long at Lake Stuart when he began to think of investigating the surrounding territory. He pushed southward and set up two more posts, one on Lake Fraser and one on the Fraser River. Still unsatisfied with this progress, he wrote to the directors of the North West Company in Montreal, asking if he might explore the Columbia River to its mouth. The Company agreed to this plan, and sent Fraser two canoes loaded with provisions and trade goods to be used on the journey.

In May 1808, he set off with two other traders and nineteen

voyageurs in four canoes, moving down what Fraser thought was the Columbia River. This was the same stream whose upper reaches had been paddled by Alexander Mackenzie in his overland dash to the Pacific. For some days Fraser and his men had little difficulty with the rapids and current of the river, but eventually they came to a place where the waters narrowed suddenly between walls of a deep canyon. The stream, swollen with the water of melting snows, boomed between the black ramparts of the dim chasm—splashing foam over fearsome rocks that rose like dark ghosts in the flying spray.

Fraser halted his canoes to look over the situation. To portage would be a long and exhausting task, but to enter the canyon might mean sudden death. Finally it was agreed that five of the best voyageurs should try to run the rapids in a lightly loaded canoe. These daredevils after pushing away from shore were caught in the vicious current, bounced over a low waterfall, and slid into the pull of a violent whirlpool which spun the canoe in dizzy circles. Round and round it went in a wild, breathless whirl so swift that the craft was a blur of movement, and then it shot across current against a low wet rock by the shore, where the men jumped frantically to solid land. Watching anxiously, Fraser sighed in relief as he saw his voyageurs scramble to safety.

With the help of neighbouring Indians and their horses, the canoes and packs were portaged about the canyon to the end of the rapids. The red men tried to persuade Fraser that he would be wiser to go overland to another and more peaceful river which flowed to the sea. The Scotsman did not realize that the stream mentioned by the Indians was the true Columbia—the river he thought he had been travelling. Had he known his real position, doubtless he would have taken the advice of the Indians.

Days later they came to another rapids so filled with whirlpools that at first glance it seemed impassable. However, the canoes were unloaded and a few daring paddlers rode the craft skilfully through the boiling waters, and then walked back to help with the packs. Carrying provisions and trading goods across the face of steep cliffs was a tough and risky task which almost ended in tragedy. One voyageur slipped off the pathway and fell into a crevice where he was wedged so tightly that he could neither climb out nor remove his pack. He was completely helpless and in a perilous position. Fraser, seeing the man's plight, risked his own life to crawl to the side of the trapped voyageur. Then, breathing heavily, the trader drew a sharp knife, cut through leather straps and let the pack go pounding down the cliff to the river below. Clawing, sliding and climbing they made their way across narrow ledges that hung dizzily over the swirling waters.

The canoe shot across the current to a low rock where the five voyageurs jumped frantically to solid land.

The grim battle with the river continued—shooting rapids, packing, dragging, climbing. They came to another canyon, too high to portage, into which they thrust their canoes and rode out the white torrent. By miraculous, good fortune all canoes escaped the seething pools, the jagged walls and the hidden rocks, to pass unharmed through this chasm of death.

Indians living below these rapids warned Fraser that he could not paddle farther down river, and this appeared to be perfectly true, for later that day they came to a stretch of water wilder and more dangerous than any they had yet seen. There was but one thing to do, and Fraser decided to do it— continue the journey by foot. After storing their canoes and a quantity of food, the men shouldered packs and began the rugged march along the river banks. As they advanced they met groups of Indians who threatened them with clubs and arrows, but Fraser on such occasions passed gifts among the tribesmen and made friends quickly.

On and on they marched past rapids and whirlpools to places where the river ran less hurriedly, and there they were able to secure dugout canoes from the Indians. Once more afloat, the voyageurs paddled swiftly down stream, but their troubles were not yet over. There were still portages to be made, and cliffs to be climbed by means of swaying wooden ladders left by the Indians.

The river swung to the westward and the rocky shores changed to low, swampy banks which were alive with mosquitoes. As the dugouts pushed through vast expanses of reeds, the explorers encountered more hostile Indians but escaped unharmed. Fraser noticed that the level of the river rose and fell as the hours passed, so he judged that he must be very close to the sea. Although he was pleased by this fact, he had come to the realization that he could not be on the Columbia River. His instruments told him that he was too far north for that. The swift, treacherous river that he had been following was one that was new and unknown to the fur traders!

They came to a place where the main course of the river divided into a number of channels which ribboned among the low islands a short distance from the open sea. Beyond that point they never passed, for war drums throbbed along the shores and the high screech of war cries drifted to the ears of the tired, ragged men in the dugouts.

In low spirits the explorers turned about and began the long paddle back up the river we now call the Fraser. They fought against the current, met Indian war parties, climbed cliffs, dragged over weary portages and tossed about on the white rapids. At one place some of the voyageurs became so downhearted and alarmed by the Indians, that they threatened to throw down their paddles and run off through the mountains. Fraser, taking stern action, made each man swear on a cross that he would not desert the party. This put fresh heart into the men and they pushed on with greater courage, at last reaching the land of the friendly Carrier Indians, where they found their own canoes and food supplies in good condition.

During early August the ragged paddlers reached New Caledonia and raised a joyful shout as they came in sight of one of the trading posts.

Although he himself was not pleased with his journey, stubborn, determined Simon Fraser had in reality made a very important discovery in the Fraser River and had completed successfully one of the most dangerous expeditions of exploration in all Canadian history.

22 DAVID THOMPSON

While Simon Fraser was accomplishing his dangerous explorations on the Pacific, a friend of his was doing a similar kind of work farther south along the coast.

The captain of the Hudson's Bay ship, *Prince Rupert,* stood on deck in the bright sunlight. His sharp eyes wandered over the rigging, down the masts and came to rest on a lad standing alone by the rail. To his first mate he said, "Who is that boy?"

"David Thompson, sir, a new apprentice in the Company, bound for Fort Churchill."

The captain pulled thoughtfully at one ear. "He's a lonely little fellow, but a bright lad, I'd say. There is intelligence in that face and determination too."

The mate nodded. "He's an orphan, sir, but has a good record with the Grey Coat School near Westminster Abbey. Very clever in mathematics, I've heard say. Poor lad, he doesn't know what is in store for him—those long dark winters, the awful loneliness of the posts, the endless forests, the desolate barrens, the scalp-snatching Indians and the ruthless Nor' Westers!" The mate shuddered.

A frown creased the captain's forehead. "Tosh, sir!" he

cried. "You don't have to be so dismal about the work of the Company. Yon lad will have a fine opportunity at Churchill. I like his looks, and I'll wager five guineas that he makes a name for himself."

Young Thompson landed at Fort Churchill, a new post near the mouth of the Churchill River which was being built to replace the old stone building, Fort Prince of Wales. The boy fitted rapidly into the life of the post and showed great ability from the very beginning.

The following year the young apprentice was transferred to York Factory near the mouth of the Nelson and there he became a post clerk, spending some of his working time in hunting rabbits and geese. He took great pleasure in studying the birds, animals, rocks and plants of the region, and much of this knowledge he recorded later in his writings.

After a year of this training he was ready for service at the inland posts which were waging a hot battle with the Nor' Westers for trade in the western fur country. In July, 1786, he was outfitted with "a trunk, a handkerchief, shoes, a gun, powder and a tin cup," and headed westward in the company of forty-six others. For the next three years he was engaged in trading with the Indians, moving from the posts to the camps, and spending a winter with the Peigans near what is now the city of Calgary.

After this period of trading Thompson was placed under the care of Philip Turner, a company surveyor, who gave the lad a thorough training in astronomy and surveying. So quick and brilliant was Thompson's progress that he was soon doing survey work on his own. During the next six years he crossed and recrossed the western lands, making surveys, recording latitude and longitude, drawing maps, charting rivers, recording distances and making numerous notes concerning the wild life and the Indian people. All his observations were made with the most painstaking care.

This was the life he loved, and as long as he was permitted to travel he was perfectly happy. However when his superiors insisted on his returning to the business of pure trade, he left the Hudson's Bay Company and took a position with the North West Company. At that time the Nor' Westers had a serious problem regarding the new western boundary dividing Canada and the United States. The international boundary had been set as the 49th parallel, but no one knew just where it fell across the western lands. It was possible, the Nor' Westers thought, that some of their trading posts might lie in American territory. Thompson was given the task of checking the boundary for some distance west, and finding the true location of the company posts.

David Thompson carried out this duty as faithfully and as skilfully as he had his work with the Hudson's Bay Company. In the course of one year he travelled two thousand miles across the prairies, checking the boundary line and locating the posts. Shortly after his return he married a pretty half-breed girl, Charlotte Small, who was fourteen years of age, and their honeymoon trip was made by canoe to Grand Portage on Lake Superior. It was after this that he began work on his famous map of the northwest, a map so thorough that it formed a basis for all future maps of the area.

Perhaps the best known of his exploration began in 1807 when he was ordered by the North West Company to establish posts in the Rockies and explore the Columbia River to its mouth. His first post, Kootenay House, was built at Windermere Lake in the southeastern part of what is now British Columbia and this became his headquarters. During the next four years he set up other posts, traded, and explored the great Columbia. This was no quick dash to the sea, but a slow and careful examination carried on with scientific exactitude.

Finally Thompson reached the Snake River, a large branch of the Columbia, and there he claimed the land in the name

David Thompson kept careful notes and records during his years of travel through the fur country. Using these, he was able to draw the first map of the Canadian West. This map was so accurate that it formed the foundation for all future maps of that area.

of England and the North West Company. Then he pushed on rapidly, and on July 15, 1811, his canoe rounded a bend in the river and the open sea lay before him. To his amazement, however, on the shore he discovered a fort and palisade made from fresh-cut logs.

In a moment there was a great shout and scramble as men poured from the fort to the water's edge, waving their arms and laughing in great delight. Here were old friends: McDougall, Stuart, Clarke, former traders of the North West Company, but now in the employ of an American trading firm.

"It's Davey Thompson," roared Stuart. "Aye, mon, but it's good to see ye! Nor' Wester or no, ye're welcome to Astoria!"

Then there followed such greetings, back-thumpings and yells as has had never been heard west of the Rockies; and to top it off came a big dinner of duck, salmon and partridge served in the little log fort.

In spite of the warm welcome he had received at the mouth of the Columbia, Thompson was disappointed that he could not claim the land for England. The Pacific Fur Company had reached the coast just two months before his arrival.

Thompson's days of exploration were over. He returned to Montreal, wrote a book of his travels called *Narrative,* and completed his big map of the northwest, including his observations with the Hudson's Bay Company and the North West Company. The map hung for some time in the banquet hall of the North West headquarters in Fort William and years later was given to the Ontario Archives in Toronto. He died near Montreal in February, 1857.

The boy who had come to Hudson Bay as a lonely orphan had indeed made a name for himself—the proud name of a great land surveyor and geographer. His maps, records and his notebooks have greatly enriched the history of Canadian exploration.

23 VILHJALMUR STEFANSSON

Although the Arctic had been explored through the centuries by such seamen as Davis, Frobisher, Baffin, Hudson, Franklin and a host of others, the polar seas still held great mysteries. After Franklin's tragic expedition the goal of Arctic explorers became the North Pole, and many expeditions failed in the quest. It was not until 1909 that an American naval officer, Admiral Peary, hoisted the Stars and Stripes over the Pole. But still the area lying to the north of Alaska and the Yukon was an unknown region. It was there that a Canadian scientist became famous for his extensive exploration and research.

During July of 1913, the *Karluk*, the *Mary Sacks* and the *Alaska* steamed out of Nome harbour and wet their bows in the summer waters of the Arctic Ocean. On deck of the *Karluk*, a thin alert man with a shock of dark hair stood watching his ships draw away from the Alaskan shore.

Although only thirty-four years of age, he was already a famous Arctic explorer, having many years' experience in the land of ice floes and flickering northern lights. He was Vilhjalmur Stefansson, a Canadian born of Icelandic parents in the province of Manitoba. If ever a man was made to challenge the Arctic wastes, it was this young scientist whose veins ran with the blood of ancient sea-rovers.

Now he was off on a summer's day to meet more adventure than a hero of fiction and more danger than a soldier of fortune.

His troubles started early. A few hours from land, the engines of the *Alaska* sputtered strangely and she was forced to turn back. Then a heavy gale struck the two remaining ships and they were separated, the *Mary Sacks* running eastward close to shore while the *Karluk* dared the open sea. It was dangerous sailing, for cargoes shifted in the holds with the lurching of the waves, causing the vessels to ride on alarming slants. Waves slopped over the bulwarks and washed churning across the decks. Frantically the crewmen worked in the dim holds, heaving and pulling the cargoes back into place.

When the gale died down, the *Mary Sacks* had disappeared and the *Karluk* was skipping eastward toward Point Barrow as pans of floating ice closed in with the relentless sureness of a circling wolf pack. The great grinding ice cakes filled in all the spaces of blue water and blocked the passage as surely as a wall of steel. The ship's captain, Bob Bartlett, moored the vessel to a large ice cake and waited developments. For a month the vessel drifted slowly westward, a lonely captive in the prison of ice.

Stefansson had good reason to believe that the ship would remain fast in the ice until the following spring, so he felt quite safe in leaving the vessel for a short hunt on shore. With four crewmen, two Eskimos, two sleds and twelve dogs, he set out in search of fresh meat for the ship's company.

A thick fog settled over the scene, blotting out the sight of the *Karluk* from the hunters ashore. When the mists faded away, Stefansson blinked his eyes in astonishment. The vessel had disappeared as if a giant magician had spread a grey cloth over the ship and whisked it away into the shadows of the Arctic.

The hunters looked at each other in dismay, and once more scanned the horizon for the dark shape of the ship. "Well," muttered Stefansson, "that's that! The icefield has broken and is carrying the *Karluk* to the westward."

Having started out with a well-equipped little fleet of three ships, the explorer was now left with two sleds and twelve dogs. To most men this would have been an overwhelming tragedy, but to Stefansson it was a minor annoyance. He worried more about his ships and crews than he did about himself. He was a man who knew the north and could live off the land if he must!

The little shore party managed to make its way to Point Barrow and on to Cape Smythe, where Stefansson reported by mail to the Canadian Government, explaining the misfortunes of his expedition, and expressing his confidence that the vessels were safe, although separated.

During the spring of 1914, Stefansson and his companions learned that the *Alaska* and the *Mary Sacks* were at Collison Point, and without delay they set off for that location. After a quick run they reached the little settlement and enjoyed a happy reunion with their comrades of the two ships.

In the meantime the *Karluk* had drifted with the icefield, westward, northwestward, southwestward to a location near Herald Island off Alaska. The vessel, still held in the jaws of ice, was being slowly crushed to death. Captain Bartlett and his crew built a small hut on the floe and stocked it with food supplies, a wise plan, for the *Karluk* drew a last agonizing breath and plunged downward into thirty-eight fathoms of water. The crew left the ship before its death dive and took shelter in their hut on the ice. Later in making their way toward shore, fourteen of the men lost their lives, and only eleven reached the safety of civilization.

In March of 1914, Stefansson left Collison Point with two men and a dog team, making his way northward over the polar

Stefansson spent five years on one expedition in the Arctic regions. Here we see him in northern clothing with one of his ships in the background. He was one explorer who could live in the Arctic by hunting and fishing.

ice. Two months later the party was in desperate straits, for the hunting had been poor and their supplies had dwindled to a dangerous point. The dogs were gnawing on old leather boots, and the men were nibbling on the last of the provisions. The spectre of starvation hung over the ice hummocks. Then a miracle happened. Stefansson shot a fat seal through the head with a well-aimed rifle bullet!

After three months of rugged, treacherous travel they reached Norway Island and there they set up a beacon to guide a ship which was to follow and pick them up. On they went to Banks Island and there they found excellent hunting, having the good fortune to shoot a number of sleek caribou. In great contentment, they cut the meat into steaks for immediate eating and set to work drying portions for winter use.

Stefansson kept watching for the ship he expected to arrive, but none put in an appearance. The men searched the shore and scanned the skyline for puffs of smoke, but no signs were found until the day Stefansson saw a fresh bootprint in the soft mud. Four miles further along the shore they came to the *Mary Sacks,* and sent up loud shouts in salute.

Seamen ran from the ship, laughing and yelling, "It's Stefansson! He's still alive!"

That winter they remained where they were, making preparations for more exploration in the spring. It was a busy time: two sleds were built from iron and wood ripped from the ship, clothing was made from furs and skins, meat was dried and packed away.

Stefansson's orders from the Canadian Government had been to explore unknown islands off the northern coast, and this task was begun in earnest during the spring of 1915. The men spread out in small parties, carrying on the careful scientific work of mapping, sounding, and recording information concerning wild life. During August, a ship, the *Polar Bear,* appeared and its officer, Captain Lane, explained that he had been sent to rescue the unfortunate explorers. Stefansson laughed aloud, saying that he and his party were not in the least of danger and could not return to civilization because they had too much work to do.

However, the next month, the *Polar Bear* did take the party northeastward to a point on Victoria Island where the men erected a house and set up winter quarters. At the south end of the big island they visited the Copper Eskimos, who were as friendly and responsive as a bunch of collie puppies.

During the spring and summer of 1916 new islands were discovered and examined with care—Borden Island, Meighen Island, Lougheed Island and others. The men accomplished amazing feats of travel and scientific observation which pleased Stefansson greatly.

The fourth winter, 1916-1917, was spent on Melville Island, lying just north of Victoria Island. The weather for months was very severe and so interfered with the work of the dog team patrols. In the spring of 1917 two men were caught in a blizzard, became lost and perished in the snows.

By the late summer of 1917 Stefansson was ready to leave that area, so preparations were made for the voyage. The *Mary Sacks* was drawn up on the beach and repaired, but when the ship was pulled back into the water by the *Polar Bear*, she appeared to be unseaworthy, so was torn down for lumber. With the help of another vessel that arrived, the *Challenge*, the expedition moved west toward Alaska. The trip was not complete before Stefansson became very ill with pneumonia and had to be taken to a hospital at Fort Yukon, where he remained a patient for three months. Even during his illness, the work of exploration went on, as men travelled the Beaufort Sea.

And so ends the story of the longest Arctic expedition on record—five years of danger, thrills and sudden death. The accomplishments of Stefansson and his companions were truly astounding, for over 90,000 square miles of land and ocean had been mapped, new islands had been discovered, and new knowledge obtained of a region and a people which until that time had lain in complete mystery.

24 HENRY LARSEN AND THE ST. ROCH

The North West Passage was finally conquered in 1906 when Roald Amundsen sailed from east to west across the top of America. It was not for another thirty-four years, however, that a ship ran the polar waters from west to east. Here is a voyage that ranks with the greatest exploits in Canadian history.

Back in 1928, workers were busy in a Vancouver shipyard, building a trim little patrol boat for the Royal Canadian Mounted Police. None of the men there realized that the ship growing under their hands was to become one of the most famous vessels in Canadian history.

When finished, there lay the *St. Roch*, as solid and sturdy a little ship as ever came out of a shipyard—one hundred and four feet from bow to stern, twenty-five feet across the beam, and drawing twelve and one-half feet of water. Her thick timbers of Douglas fir were enclosed in a coat of Australian iron-bark, a wood so tough it could withstand the awful pressure of grinding ice.

Her first skipper was a clever seaman, Sergeant Henry Larsen, who was to become as famous as the *St. Roch* herself. For twelve years they sailed together from Vancouver, around

Alaska and as far east as King William's Land, engaged in the task of freighting supplies to police posts scattered along the bleak shores. They battled heaving waters, snow, hail, shrieking winds and ice floes, sometimes being frozen in for whole winters near lonely coastal posts.

Then in 1940 came a breathtaking opportunity for the little patrol boat and her dauntless captain. Officials of the R.C.M.P. wanted to know if Henry Larsen and the *St. Roch* would care to sail the North West Passage across the top of America! Would they?

They certainly would! Just when would they start?

Although Henry Larsen accepted the offer quickly, he fully realized the risk he took in pitting his tiny schooner against the power of the Arctic seas. He knew that in all history at least one hundred and fifty expeditions had tried to conquer the awesome Passage, and that in four hundred and fifty years only one ship had made its way through this graveyard of exploration. He knew the story of Sir John Franklin who had disappeared into the Arctic in 1845, and of the forty-two expeditions that had combed the ice floes for signs of his party. He knew that the Passage had been beaten by only one man, Roald Amundsen, who sailed from the Atlantic to the Pacific, in 1903-1906.

When the *St. Roch* was ready for the voyage, she was loaded down with an astounding cargo of one hundred and fifty tons of freight lashed to her decks and stored in her hold. Part of these supplies were for the expedition itself and part for the Mounted Police stations strung like beads along the northern coast.

On June 18, 1940, the little vessel left Vancouver harbour, steamed between Vancouver Island and the mainland, and pointed her nose northward toward Alaska. The crew members, selected from the ranks of the R.C.M.P., were not trained sailors and soon became violently seasick as the ship ran into heavy weather. Big waves dashed over the *St. Roch's* decks, making it impossible for the cook to use the galley-stove. For a time they had to live on cold sandwiches.

Through Bering Strait she sailed and on into the Arctic Ocean, meeting ice floes for the first time. On the northern shores of Yukon Territory the *St. Roch* anchored for two weeks

VOYAGE OF THE ST. ROCH

while some supplies were transferred from her hold to that of another R.C.M.P. vessel, the *Aklavik*. By August 28, the *St. Roch* was steaming eastward toward Coppermine where a number of sleigh dogs were picked up. As the voyage continued the unfortunate dogs became seasick and added their howls to the song of the wind in the rigging.

By the end of October they were frozen in at Walker Bay,

and Larsen made rapid preparations for the long winter that lay ahead. The men cut ice, set some fish nets, spread a canvas windbreak about the ship, and began to train the sleigh dogs for patrol duties. By radio Larsen received orders from R.C.M.P. headquarters as to his winter work. He and his men were expected to carry out the regular tasks of the northern Mounties: visiting Eskimo villages, providing hungry natives with food, reporting ice conditions and examining harbours.

They spent a lonely Christmas day, December 25, 1940, but were cheered in the evening by hearing radio messages from their families and friends at home. Spring finally came with a welcome relief, but it was nearly the end of July before the *St. Roch* was moved from the grip of the ice. By blasting with gun powder and ramming the floes, they made their way slowly from the bay and pushed on toward the east.

A month later they were in sight of King William coast, but the weather and ice conditions were so miserable they made slow headway. They fought screaming winds and grinding ice fields while heavy fogs and drenching rains dropped from grey skies. After seven days of grim battle they were stopped by ice in Pasley Bay on the Peninsula of Boothia not far from the North Magnetic Pole. Larsen was disappointed by the short distance travelled that summer, and reported to headquarters that weather conditions had been unusually bad throughout the Arctic. Heavy winds had kept the pack ice close to shore, making rapid sailing impossible.

That winter they spent as they had the one before, patrolling the coast and visiting Eskimo settlements. After another lonely Christmas, sudden tragedy struck on board the *St. Roch,* when Constable Chartrand died suddenly of a heart attack one evening after dinner. The saddened crew ripped boards from the ship, made a rough coffin and buried the constable below a pile of grey stones on the cold shore.

Near King William's Land the "St. Roch" fought screaming winds and grinding ice-floes. Compare this little vessel with the sailing ships on page 130 and page 156.

Almost four months later, a Catholic priest, Father Henry, read the burial ceremony on the deck of the *St. Roch*. Henry Larsen and one of his men had made a thousand-mile overland dash to a lonely mission station to secure the priest for the funeral service! Their own lives were almost lost in the dangerous trek.

By August 3, 1942, the *St. Roch* was once again pushing strongly against summer ice and finally freed herself to take up her long struggle with the Arctic seas. Northward she made her way around Baffin Island and into Baffin Bay. The worst of the Passage lay behind, but sudden disaster lurked ahead in Davis Strait, a waterway darkly famous for its treacherous icebergs. Through the long days and the dark nights they kept a constant watch, searching for the giant icebergs as they crept through cold fogs and bouncing fields of ice.

Finally they passed out of Davis Strait, entered the Atlantic and came to Bateau Harbour on the coast of Labrador, where they cheered at the sight of a fishing schooner. A little better than two weeks later they arrived at Sydney, Nova Scotia, and after a short stop pushed on to the final goal.

On October 11, 1942, the battered little ship entered the harbour of Halifax and eased up to the dock. The cruel grip of the Arctic ice lay far behind; the peace and security of the big seaport lay close at hand.

The startling news of the two-year voyage across the top of the continent was flashed across the world by radio, telegraph and telephone. Newspapers came out with big headlines. The last chapter in the long history of the North West Passage was now complete—the voyage from west to east had been made!

The gallant *St. Roch* was not yet through with the Arctic, however, for almost two years later, in 1944, she made the return trip from Halifax to Vancouver, making the long voyage of seven thousand two hundred and ninety-five miles in eighty-six days. Although this was a very rapid trip, it was not without adventure. Off Yukon Territory the little vessel ran into a hurricane which almost wrecked her and later off the coast of Alaska she just missed being trapped by closing ice packs. Henry Larsen and the *St. Roch* had sailed the North West Passage both ways!

Six years later under the command of Sergeant Farrar, the *St. Roch* left Vancouver, sailed southward, passed through the Panama Canal and steamed northward to Halifax in 1950. The wonder ship had created another record. She was the first ship in history to circle the North American continent!

The deeds of the *St. Roch*, Henry Larsen and his magnificent crew illustrate the quiet but brilliant work which is being accomplished continuously by the men of the famous Royal Canadian Mounted Police.

25 SIR FRANCIS DRAKE

In 1513 Nunez de Balboa had claimed the Pacific for the Spanish King, but sixty-four years later a dashing English sea rover invaded this ocean and gave much trouble to the astonished Spaniards.

When the hurricane had blown itself out, and the mighty waves of the Gulf of Mexico had fallen to a low roll, Francis Drake looked over his ship.

"Look alive, you men," he bellowed, "check the hull and rigging. I want to know what the damage is."

When Drake's ships and the others in the little British fleet were examined, it was found that the pounding of the sea and the lashing of the wind had battered the vessels into a pitiful state.

Drake was furious. "What beastly luck!" he raged. "Here we are lying off Spanish lands with a broken fleet. There is nothing else for it—Sir John will have to ask leave to dock in Vera Cruz. What a sad position for an English sea-dog!"

The young captain was right, for his commander, Sir John Hawkins, sent a messenger to the Spanish Viceroy and received permission to repair his vessels in the harbour of Vera Cruz.

In the humid heat of the port, the seamen went to work, some ashore and others climbing like monkeys in the rigging.

Francis Drake, mopping his sweating face, watched the activity of the harbour. Across the waters he could see Spaniards loading frigates with small heavy boxes that bent the shoulders of the workers. He leaned forward, squinting his eyes, in an effort to gain a clearer view of the loading. "I wonder," he muttered, "I wonder if that could be gold . . . small packages . . . heavy in weight . . . very interesting indeed!"

The English sailors were busily engaged with their repairs when the Spanish launched a treacherous attack that caught the visitors by surprise. It came with speed and fury. Spanish fire-ships, crackling and blazing, roared down on the anchored British fleet. A cannon boomed and a ball whistling across English decks struck a drinking cup from the hands of John Hawkins. With an exclamation of surprise, the commander, dressed in full armour, somersaulted backward into the sea. On shore the Spaniards with naked swords leaped on the defenceless Englishmen, cutting them down in cold blood.

Drake dashed across the deck of his vessel, screamed orders, cut ropes and headed for the sea. Hawkins was not far behind, for he seized a loose rope in the water, with a heroic effort clambered over the side of a ship, and in a short time whipped the vessel out of the harbour.

Both Drake and Hawkins reached England in safety, but memories of the Spanish attack lingered in their minds. A few years later young Drake, like a dashing pirate, was back in the Gulf of Mexico, capturing treasure ships, and looting towns along the Spanish colonies. By 1572 he was marching across the Isthmus of Panama to the Pacific Ocean, and there for the first time he viewed the western sea. Standing in a tree top, Drake scanned the broad waters and a pleased smile broke across his face. "There it lies," he murmured, "the sea the Spanish call their own. If heaven permits, I'll float a good English ship on those waters and trade cannon balls with any who dare to stop me!"

Francis Drake returned to England a very wealthy man, since a fortune in Spanish gold was stored below the decks of his ship. With the Pacific still in mind, he had five ships built for his next expedition and with these he set out for the southern seas. On board his own flagship, the *Pelican*, he lived like a king. Ten young waiters of noble birth hurried to serve his meals on plates of solid gold, while musicians played dinner music on violins and harps. Dressed in suits of finest velvet and shirts of gleaming linen, the captain dined heartily on rich foods and sipped expensive wines from distant lands.

The *Pelican* led her brood southwestward across the Atlantic to the coast of Brazil, and there two of the small craft were emptied of their stores and left near the river Plata. By August 1577, the three remaining vessels were fighting their way through the Strait of Magellan, pitching on violent waves churned up by cutting winds. Only one vessel survived the horrible passage, and that was the gallant *Pelican*. Pleased with the performance of his sturdy ship, Drake renamed her the *Golden Hind*.

Having reached the Pacific, Drake turned northward, following the long coastline of Chile and eventually came to the port of Valparaiso. With the help of an Indian, picked up along the coast, the *Golden Hind* was run into the harbour, where treasure ships lay peacefully at anchor. Spanish seamen, thinking Drake's ship one of their own, waved in friendly salute and calmly went on with their work.

The situation was so perfect from Drake's standpoint that he hid a grim smile in his dark beard. He gave a signal and the swift attack began as the *Golden Hind* hooked quickly to a treasure ship with grappling-irons. English seamen leaped the bulwarks, shouting and waving cutlasses, as they drove

the Spaniard down the open hatches or over the side into the
sea. Cannon on the deck of the *Golden Hind* lashed out at the
other treasure ships, smashing rigging, sails and hulls. The
shocked Spaniards were overcome in a few minutes' time and
their ships fell into English hands. Laughing Englishmen
emptied the holds of their precious cargoes and pushed the
crewless vessels out to sea.

This was just the beginning of Drake's swift raids on the
west coast of South America, since other ports and towns were

*The "Golden Hind" fired at the Spanish treasure ship, knocking her sails into
the sea. Notice how the sailing vessels of those days were high in the bow
and stern, but low in the middle section.*

to feel the sting of the *Golden Hind*. From some captured seamen, Drake heard of a famous treasure ship, the *Glory of the Southern Seas*, which was on the ocean carrying an enormous shipment of gold from the colonies to Spain.

"*Glory of the Southern Seas!*" roared Drake joyfully. "Now there's a prize to fight for!"

The hunt began, and day and night it continued with lookouts scanning the seas from the rigging of the *Golden Hind*. Then one afternoon about three o'clock, the cry "Sail ho!" rang out from away above the deck, and seamen rushed to their battle stations.

The *Glory of the Southern Seas* was sailing slowly and peacefully southward, and then to Drake's astonishment she lowered sail and came almost to a standstill. Thinking the *Golden Hind* was a friendly vessel bearing orders from the Viceroy, the Spanish captain waited quite innocently for the arrival of the pursuing ship.

The *Golden Hind*, dashing in toward the treasure ship, let go with thirty blazing cannon that knocked masts, rigging and sails crashing into the sea. Grappling irons were thrust over the bulwarks, and English seamen charged across the decks with swords flashing circles in the air. The helpless Spaniards, not felled by the first charge, surrendered quickly and yielded up the *Glory of the Southern Seas*.

When the cargo of the treasure ship was loaded on the *Golden Hind*, Drake's ship rode low in the water, heavy with the weight of gold. There was no need now for more raids; the quest was over and it was time to go home. Even the dauntless Drake dared not return to the Atlantic with an overloaded ship, so he ordered a northern course, hoping that he might find a passage leading eastward through North America.

It is not known how far north he sailed, but he did reach the coast of what is now California, and he claimed the land in the name of Queen Elizabeth of England. Drake was discouraged by the fact that the coastline of the continent swung to the west rather than the east as he had hoped. Regretfully he decided that North America must reach almost to Asia in the far north and that no great waterway flowed eastward to the Atlantic. His guess was surprisingly accurate, as we know today, but this was not proved until the voyages of Captain James Cook, two centuries later.

Drake turned his ship's bow to the southwest, crossed the Pacific, reached the East Indies, pushed over the Indian Ocean, rounded the tip of Africa and headed eagerly for home.

In September, 1580, the *Golden Hind*, travel-worn and battered, sailed into the harbour of Plymouth to the wild cheers of her happy crew. After an absence of almost three years the tired vessel slid to the wharf and her barnacled timbers creaked a sigh of relief.

It was a heroes' welcome for Francis Drake and the crew of the *Golden Hind*. In the long course of British history few men have been received home with the same wild burst of admiration.

At the inns and coffee shops across Britain, farmers, merchants and labourers discussed the startling news and thumped their fists on oak tables to express their feelings. " 'E done it!" they shouted, " 'e fought the Spaniards in their own seas, and snatched their gold from beneath their noses! Here's to Francis Drake—the greatest seaman of them all!"

Queen Elizabeth, to show her pleasure, dined on board the *Golden Hind* and listened to vivid tales of the southern seas. After the pleasant affairs of the long dinner were over, she commanded Drake to kneel before her. Then touching his shoulder lightly with a sword, she said, "Rise, Sir Francis Drake."

Another chapter of discovery in the distant Americas was complete.

26 THE SPANISH IN CALIFORNIA

The Spanish, alarmed by the activity of British and Russian seamen, decided to occupy land on the Pacific lying north of the colony in Mexico.

A tall thin secretary in the Spanish Viceregal palace of Mexico City handed a package to the Viceroy and bowed. "Your Excellency," he said, "this is a royal despatch just received from Spain."

Quickly the Viceroy broke the seal and opened the bulky papers. He settled himself in his high-backed chair, crossed his knees, pursed his lips and commenced to read the King's mail.

When he had finished, he lay the papers aside and exclaimed, "Good! We are going to move into California! It's time too, now that the Russians and the English have been poking their noses into the Pacific. Unless we act soon, those Russians will sweep down from Alaska and take up the whole coast. As for the English—Heaven preserve us—we never know what they are up to!"

The secretary bowed once more. "Very good, your Excellency, will there be any messages?"

"Yes! Yes, indeed, there will be messages. We must get a letter off to De Galvez right away, asking him to organize an expedition. Yes indeed, right away. There is no time to be lost. We must start soldiers marching and ships sailing. Coasts must be explored; harbours must be opened; forts must be built, missions must be founded. Good news, indeed! Wonderful news! Long live the King of Spain!"

And so it was that the Spanish moved into California to prevent possible invasion by the Russians or by the English. In 1769, vessels sailed northward and troops marched overland from Spanish ports in the peninsula of Lower California which was already in Spanish hands. In a few months' time small groups were at San Diego and at Monterey, setting up forts for the garrisons. Missions, too, were built under the leadership of a very active man, Father Serra, who had been placed in charge of all religious work in California.

In the beginning there was some difficulty in keeping the new posts supplied with food, but as time went on, conditions improved and soldiers spread farther up the coast. A naval base was built at San Blas, and three new mission stations were opened at San Antonio, San Gabriel and San Luis Obispo.

Five years after the founding of the first military posts a land route was opened between what is now Arizona and the Californian coast, when a group of twenty-one soldiers made the long, tiresome journey overland. The opening of the land route was closely followed by the founding of San Francisco which lay far to the north of the other posts.

Until 1777, the Spanish ports in California had been peopled by priests and soldiers; no settlers had yet arrived to set up homes and till the soil. However, in that year the Viceroy commanded the Governor of California to start a programme of settlement by which real settlers would be brought into the country. The first of these made the hard journey overland, taking with them herds of animals for their

When the Spaniards moved northward from Mexico and into California, they set up mission stations and forts along the coast. In this picture we see a new mission under construction. Notice the men cutting lumber with a cross-cut saw.

future farms. Fourteen families founded the little settlement of San José, and in 1781, another eleven families started a second settlement which was to become the city of Los Angeles.

Not all the settlers who had started out for Los Angeles reached their goal, for the discontented Yuma Indians had attacked the party, killing a number of priests, soldiers and settlers. Spanish vengeance fell swiftly on the Yumas, for two bands of soldiers hurried into the Indian lands, killed two hundred red men and released some Spanish captives.

The work of setting up more missions and founding new settlements continued rapidly. Father Serra had for some time been anxious to send missionaries among the powerful Indians living along the Santa Barbara channel to the north of Los Angeles, and this was done when sufficient soldiers were on hand to protect the priests.

When the Santa Barbara district was occupied, the Spanish were spread along the coast for over five hundred miles between the peninsula of Lower California and San Francisco. Four large forts were spaced in such a way that they protected groups of small missions. As the years went by, more and more missions were established by Father Serra until there were twenty-one of them scattered along the coast and inland through the valleys. These little missions became prosperous communities with farms, ranches, herds and orchards. The priests worked among the Indians converting them to Christianity and teaching them how to farm and take part in other occupations. Bells rang across the neat fields of the green valleys as lines of Indian men, women and children made their way to beautiful white chapels on the hill tops.

Father Serra, who had been the organizer of all this remarkable activity, died in the year 1784.

Such was the birth of California, a lovely land which still bears the mark of the Spanish soldier, the Spanish settler and the Spanish priest.

27 CAPTAIN JAMES COOK

While the Spanish were moving to California, farther north a great English navigator was roving the Pacific and exploring American shores.

In a London dining-room tobacco smoke floated like a blue mist before burning candles that reflected soft lights from tall crystal goblets, plates of fine china, and pieces of sterling silver. Gentlemen in wigs and velvet coats, officers in naval uniforms, puffed their pipes and talked among themselves.

A gruff old admiral with a white beard turned to a friend and spoke in a whisper. "Who is to command this Royal Navy expedition in search of a North West Passage?"

His friend shrugged his shoulders. "Who knows? The navy has ships, men, provisions and equipment, but no leader."

"What!" snorted the admiral, "an expedition without a leader? Preposterous!"

"Now, now, Admiral, don't get excited. There will be a leader, but he has not been chosen yet by the Admiralty. I have no doubt that . . ."

"Sh!" said the admiral.

A tall handsome man in a grey wig and naval uniform

had risen to his feet, and was about to address the gathering. "My lords and gentlemen," he began, "if it pleases the Admiralty, I shall be willing to command the forthcoming expedition."

There was an immediate roar of applause and shouts of approval from the men.

"Capital!" bellowed the old admiral as he thumped the table. "Captain James Cook . . . not a better seaman in England . . . sounded the St. Lawrence . . . fought with Wolfe at Quebec . . . charted the coasts of Newfoundland and Labrador . . . sailed below the Antarctic Circle . . . beat the disease of scurvy . . . twice around the world . . . what a navigator! By thunder, if there is a North West Passage, James Cook will find it!"

                                ❊   ❊   ❊

Captain Cook was given two vessels, the *Resolution* and the *Discovery,* and these were stored with a queerly assorted cargo of provisions, trade supplies, grains, seeds, pigs, goats, geese, chickens and a few cows. The sturdy ships were outfitted, too, with the best instruments of the time for the study of astronomy and the practice of navigation.

According to his orders, Cook started southward from England in the summer of 1776 and made his way slowly to the tip of Africa, crossed the Indian Ocean to the East Indies and then turned northeastward to a group of islands which he named the Sandwich Islands. Today we know them as Hawaii.

After a short stop, the vessels pushed on and in March, 1778, came in sight of what is now the coast of California, a place which had been claimed for England years before by the great Elizabethan sea dog, Sir Francis Drake. A landing on the coast was prevented by an inconsiderate storm which drove the vessels northward to the west side of Vancouver

Island. There in a magnificent setting they landed at Nootka Sound.

The Indians of the island, completely unafraid of the visitors, leaped nimbly into dugout canoes and paddled

At Nootka Sound the Indians paddled in dugout canoes to meet the ships of Captain Cook. Notice the beautiful curved shape of the Indian canoes. The Indians of the west coast were clever artists and wood carvers.

toward the ships. Captain Cook never forgot that amazing scene with great mountain ridges rising to the clouds, the snowy peak of Mount Baker in the distance, the twisted roots of cypress trees by the waterside, long ribbons of Spanish moss swaying in the branches; and before that vivid backdrop came the fleet of painted canoes, their high carved prows rising like miniature totem poles.

The British seamen spent an enjoyable month at Nootka and during that time they engaged in a brisk fur trade with the Indians. Trading was not a new experience to these tribesmen for Russians and others had been coming to these waters to secure the beautiful sea-otter skins. Although Cook's men were not well prepared for trade, they found that the red men were quite happy to give up their pelts in exchange for any bits of metal. Brass rings, candlesticks, belt buckles, tin mirrors and even old rusty nails were handed over hurriedly for the soft, glossy skins of the sea-otter.

The men of the crews became so excited by the ease and wealth of the fur trade that they did not want to go on with the task of exploring the coast. It appeared to them that they could make more money in sea-otters than they could by winning the British prize of 20,000 pounds offered for the discovery of the North West Passage.

By May 1, Cook managed to get his men aboard the ships and started northward along the coast, exploring and charting the inlets of the shoreline, always hoping to find a passage leading eastward across the continent. Gradually the coasts of what are now British Columbia and Alaska were inspected, and the ships finally arrived at Bering Strait, a narrow stretch of water separating America from Asia. It was impossible, Cook discovered then, to proceed farther, for the way was blocked by a solid ice-field.

It must be remembered that Captain Cook was not the first to sail these waters, for Vitus Bering, flying the Russian flag, had reached Alaska thirty-seven years before. Cook's expedition, however, was the more important of the two for his careful records and observations proved several things: first, that Asia and America were separated by a narrow strait;

second, that Alaska was part of America; third, that no great waterway passed through the heart of America.

Satisfied that his long exploration of the Pacific coast was complete, Cook left the northern waters and sailed for the Sandwich Islands. He planned to spend the winter there repairing his ships and exploring among the islands.

Cook and his seamen were delighted with the green islands, the warm climate and the friendly natives. At first the crews and the islanders were on the very best of terms, but this ceased when Cook allowed his men to cut timber near the native burial grounds. This breaking of a *taboo* caused resentment on the part of the natives. They became sullen and hostile. Feeling between the two groups grew tense, as native women and children were kidnapped and taken aboard the vessels; in revenge the islanders stole a rowboat from the *Discovery*.

This serious situation was climaxed by the shooting of a chief and a sharp skirmish in the shallow waters along the beach. As Cook turned his back on the shore to signal his men, a knife blade was plunged into his back and he fell forward into the sea. Screaming natives fell on him, striking and stabbing at the struggling figure . . . the salt water turned crimson and Cook lay still.

Hours after the savage encounter, the Captain's battered body was recovered by the seamen, and on February 21, 1779, during an impressive funeral service, the great navigator was dropped over the ship's side and into the depths of the Pacific Ocean.

The news of Captain Cook's long voyage and tragic death spread through Europe and Asia, causing a fresh interest to arise in the Pacific coast of America. Traders, merchants, seamen and kings turned their eyes greedily on the beautiful land of the sea-otter.

28 CAPTAIN GEORGE VANCOUVER

With the English and the Spanish both sailing the waters of the Pacific Ocean it was inevitable that the two nations should clash over land rights in America. One of the first quarrels was over land on what is now Vancouver Island.

Two old men, one a soldier and the other a sailor, sat on the docks of Liverpool, watching the lazy movements of sailing vessels and the swift dive of seagulls in the blue sky. Their days of fighting and sailing were long past—now they were content to sit in the warm sunshine, smoke their pipes and whittle soft wood with their pocket knives.

The wrinkled, old tar shoved back his hat from his forehead and looked at his friend. "Do ye think we'll be fighting the Spaniards again?" he asked.

"Aye," replied the soldier, "there be no doubt of that. Look what those thievin' Spaniards are doing in the Pacific. This English seaman, John Meares, gets a little fort built at Nootka Sound to trade in sea-otters, and then along comes a Spanish fleet from San Francisco. And what do they do? Why, they just sail, proud as dukes, into Nootka, take Meare's fort, and seize his vessels! Piracy—that's what it is! I tell ye, John, old England can't stand for the like of that!"

With a quick nod of his head, the sailor thrust a crooked finger and jabbed at his friend. "Ye're right! It's time to strike when they're seizing English ships and English property! We whipped the Spaniards in the days of Francis Drake, and we'll do it again!"

Back in that year of 1790, it appeared as if the two old men were right about war breaking out between England and

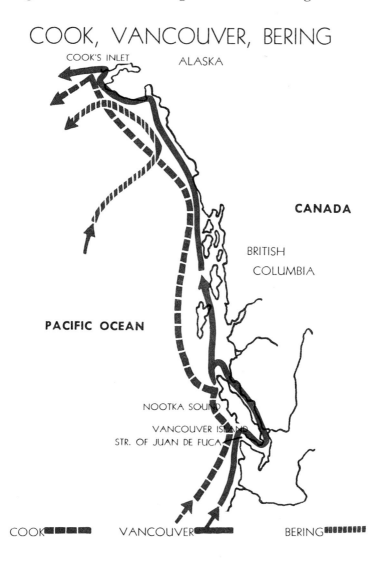

COOK, VANCOUVER, BERING

COOK'S INLET ALASKA

CANADA

BRITISH
COLUMBIA

PACIFIC OCEAN

NOOTKA SOUND

VANCOUVER ISLAND
STR. OF JUAN DE FUCA

COOK ▬▬▬▬   VANCOUVER ▬▬▬   BERING ▐▐▐▐▐▐▐▐

Spain over the affair of John Meares, English seaman in the sea-otter trade. Alarmed by the arrival of Americans, Russians and British in the "Spanish Ocean," Spain had captured a British fort and vessels at Nootka Sound. Such bold action, of course, threw England into such a state of anger that her seamen were quite ready to take vengeance on the Spanish raiders.

In spite of this dangerous situation, war did not come. Spain was not strong enough to fight England's powerful navy and army, so that the matter was settled by an agreement called the "Nootka Convention." By this, Spain agreed to repay John Meares for his losses, and to hand back the Nootka lands.

In order to settle the details of the agreement it was decided that an English expedition should be sent to Nootka Sound to talk with the Spanish there. Captain George Vancouver, the commander, was a seaman of long and famous experience. As a young midshipman he had sailed with Captain James Cook, and had been with the great navigator when he was killed by the natives in the Sandwich Islands. Vancouver was going back to Nootka for a second time.

He left England in April, 1791, with two ships, the *Discovery* and the *Chatham*, sailing southward around Africa, on to Australia, and northeastward across the Pacific toward America. A little more than a year after leaving home, he came in sight of the northern coast; near Vancouver Island he was startled to meet an American ship which was exploring and trading in those waters. Vancouver talked with its captain, Robert Gray, and learned that the American had discovered the mouth of a great river which he named in honour of his vessel, the *Columbia*.

After some exploration of the Strait of Juan de Fuca, Vancouver sailed on to Nootka Sound on the west coast of the island, where he found a Spanish officer, Don Quadra,

Vancouver's seamen fired a salute in honour of the Spanish party at Nootka Sound. Notice the costumes of the two British officers and of the seamen who are firing the gun.

waiting for him. It is difficult to imagine what thoughts the two commanders held at the time of the meeting. Whatever they may have been, the men greeted each other like brothers. Both Spanish and English cannon boomed salutes from the decks of the ships, and a great deal of good gun powder was wasted in the welcome ceremony. Don Quadra, with polished Spanish manners, entertained Vancouver and his officers to a remarkable five-course banquet which made British eyes grow round.

This was just the beginning of a series of entertainments and dinners which were held on shore and aboard the vessels. Indians sang songs and performed dances; seamen swung through jigs and reels to the music of fife and drum; fireworks shot into the dark skies from the decks of British ships.

Don Quadra remained so friendly and helpful that Captain Vancouver gained a true liking and respect for the Spanish gentleman. They became good friends, dining together daily, but they never did settle the matter for which they had been sent to Nootka. Vancouver insisted that Spain should surrender all the region about Nootka, while Don Quadra was agreeable only to giving up a small patch of land on which John Meares' fort had stood. The talks went on and on, with neither side giving in.

Unable to come to any agreement, the two commanders left Nootka on friendly terms, hoping that the problem would be solved by the home governments. Such was the case, for three years later it was decided in Europe that Spain would give up the Nootka district to England.

Vancouver's work on the Pacific was not yet completed, as he had been commanded to make a careful exploration of the coast from California to Alaska. This was a staggering task, but the navigator tackled it with such energy that he actually examined the shoreline from San Francisco north to Cook's Inlet in Alaska. From 1792 to 1794 he stuck at the tedious work of sounding, exploring and charting the lonely waters.

One of the discoveries made by the expedition was that the large island now bearing the name of Vancouver was separated from the coast of America by a navigable channel. Up until that time the seamen and traders had believed that it was part of the mainland.

Before the survey was completed, the long days of exposure to the cold and the sea had begun to take effect on Vancouver's health—he became a victim of tuberculosis. Nevertheless, he finished his explorations, and then made the long voyage back to England, where he busied himself writing the record of his travels and completing his charts of the Pacific coast of America.

Captain George Vancouver, like his former commander, James Cook, had given his life in the cause of British exploration. He died in England when only forty years of age, but the names of an island and a city on the beautiful west coast of Canada still remind us of him.

29 THE GOLD RUSH TO CALIFORNIA

Numbers of American merchants, traders, ranchers and adventurers gradually moved into the Spanish lands of California, setting up homes, businesses and ranches. As the years went by, they became discontented with Mexican rule, and rebelled against it, forming a country of their own called the Republic of California. In 1848, however, the Republic joined the United States and became the State of California.

In the Valley of Sacramento, northeast of San Francisco, lay the rolling acres of a ranch, stretching for miles across the beautiful countryside to the foothills of the mountains. Its owner, John Sutter, lived like a lord in a huge house surrounded by a palisade and protected by a garrison of soldiers. From the walls of the "fort" he could see his herds of cattle and horses grazing on the ranges or trotting in bunches before the sweep of shouting cowboys.

In 1847, Sutter decided to build a mill to make lumber from the trees that grew in plenty along the mountain slopes; being a man of action, he gave orders for construction, sending off a group of workers under a man called Marshall.

Marshall discovered an excellent place for a mill, where a

swift stream, passing through the forest on the way down the mountain, turned in a splendid curve. As the building grew, the workers dug a deep ditch in the stream bed to provide space for the big mill wheel. They splashed about in the water, swinging their shovels, throwing sand and stones to the banks.

Marshall, watching one day, was startled to see small specks of yellow substance shining from the piles of dirt. Quickly he gathered up a number of the tiny particles and turned them over and over in his hand. Then, taking one of the larger pieces, he pounded it out on a rock—it spread into a thin glowing sheet that held together in one piece. Marshall's fingers trembled in excitement as he filled a tin plate with gravel and washed away the gritty dirt with water from the stream. A quick breath burst from his lips, as he saw more of the shiny bits clinging to the bottom of the grimy plate, like stars in a wintry sky.

Leaping to his feet, he waved his arms wildly. "Hey, you fellows," he yelled, "I think we've struck gold!"

The workmen, leaving their jobs, rushed to Marshall's side, jostling each other in an effort to see the shining bits in the tin plate. Some of the men swore it was gold, but others laughed loudly, making a joke of Marshall's discovery.

Some days later, Marshall rode to the ranch house, carrying with him a small bag of the metal particles to show to Sutter. Arriving at the house late at night, he hurried to talk with the ranch owner. Secretly the two of them put the metal to all the tests they knew, and finally were convinced that the glittering bits were true gold.

Sutter's eyes snapped with the thrill of the find. "Just think of it, Marshall," he sputtered, "gold scattered all over this ranch! Bags and bags of it!"

Then his eyes narrowed in thought. "But look here, man," he added hurriedly, "we've got to keep this thing quiet, or

These big covered wagons with canvas tops jiggled and squeaked across the badlands, the prairies and the mountains, on the way to the west coast.

we'll have hundreds of men pouring into California, rushing around like fools, digging up the streams and hills!"

Marshall nodded his head in agreement.

In spite of their efforts to keep the secret, the news of gold spread across California to San Francisco, and from there it moved slowly to the eastern part of the United States. Bedlam broke loose as men by the thousands left their homes and businesses to hurry across the continent to the alluring gold fields. Even Marshall and Sutter never guessed what a wild, colourful, staggering stampede it was to be! Covered wagons, men on horses, men on mules and men on two feet plodded over the prairies under the lash of winds and storms to the Rockies and on to California. The main flood of the rush came in 1849, and for this reason the miners are often called Forty-Niners.

Men in full-sailed schooners, slim clipper ships, worm-eaten old vessels left the harbours of the Atlantic coast to sail to Panama where they travelled overland and boarded other vessels sailing north. Some of the craft made the long voyage about Cape Horn and scudded along the South American coast, and on to San Francisco. The long sleek clippers sailed like gulls; the fat water-logged ships wallowed like wounded ducks in the heavy seas.

San Francisco grew from a struggling little settlement to a sprawling city marked by cluttered patches of tents, ricketty huts and board shacks. Not all the newcomers were true miners, for among them were ruffians, criminals, bandits and gamblers who turned the city into as wild and lawless a place as ever existed in the New World. Honest miners were robbed of their gold, gun fights broke out in the streets and gambling flourished in the saloons and dance halls. There was no law in the land of gold, no policemen, no jails, no judges, and only when the honest men grouped themselves into bands of "vigilantes" was some sort of order and peace brought to the roaring city.

Miners arriving by land or sea rushed with their picks and shovels to the busy diggings that lay along the rivers and streams. Standing on the banks or deep in the cold waters, they dug, swirled their pans and poured the gleaming gold dust into leather pouches. In the early days of the rush hundreds of miners washed from twenty-five to fifty dollars worth of dust each day. Six hundred million dollars worth was taken from the streams during the first twelve years of activity. After that, most of the surface gold was gone, so the chances of making fortunes became fewer and fewer.

As the gold dwindled, thousands of the miners began making their way back to their homes across the United States, and the city of San Francisco became almost a ghost town. Some of the miners, however, remained in the country and took up farming and other forms of work which, in many cases, proved more profitable than the gold fields.

Ranches, little settlements, churches and schools made their appearance across the countryside. California became so important that it was necessary to find swifter means of transportation between it and the eastern states. Concord coaches, painted in bright colours and drawn by six horses, dashed across the country with passengers, mail and freight, daring blizzards, landslides, Indians and highwaymen. Even these swiftly moving stages became too slow for mail service and the famous pony express was founded by which mail pouches were whisked from the railway line on the Mississippi over the mountains to the Pacific. Daring horsemen galloped at breakneck speeds along rough trails from post to post, changing horses every twenty miles, to speed off across deserts, plains and mountains.

These were the forerunners of the great busses, the luxurious trains, and the sleek planes that now speed between the East and the cities of modern California.

30   THE CARIBOO TRAIL

In 1857, gold was discovered in the Fraser valley of what is now British Columbia, setting off a second mad rush. Miners left California and hurried northward in sailing vessels. Victoria, a tiny settlement on Vancouver Island was overwhelmed by twenty thousand people who camped in tents outside the walls of the Hudson's Bay post.

The fur trader leaned forward as he spoke to Governor James Douglas. "Did you ever see anything like it?" he cried. "Thousands and thousands of them pouring in here, all crazy with the fever for gold! I tell you what, I look back on the days of fur trading with envy. Those were the days when a man had time to think! Right now Victoria is all in an uproar with men wanting picks, shovels, pans, flour, bacon, beans, coffee, boots and tobacco . . . men wanting rides to the mainland on Company boats . . . men wanting this . . . men wanting that!"

James Douglas stroked his long sidewhiskers. "You think you have troubles?" he asked. "What about me? Here I am, Governor of a British colony, with an army of American miners on my hands—tough, wild fellows packing guns on their hips!"

The fur trader chuckled. "What are you worrying about?

You have done a fine job of handling the rush. You clapped a mining tax on these strangers, and you warned them there would be no lawlessness here. You told them British justice would be carried out!"

"That's right," agreed Douglas. "I warned them and I meant what I said. Judges will hold court in the mining country and men who break the law will be punished. There will be no wild-west nonsense here!"

The bold words of James Douglas were no idle boast, for the gold rush of the Fraser was a very peaceful affair compared with the roaring days of the California stampede.

By the spring of 1858, companies of miners in hobnailed boots were surging up the Fraser River in steamers, old sailing ships, canoes and rowboats. Along the shores others made their way on foot, in wagons, on horseback—climbing, slipping in the wet mud and over slippery rocks. The river, swollen by the heavy snows of winter, ran deep, covering many of the sandbars that the men had hoped to work. By late summer, however, the level of the river had gone down, and mining began in earnest.

The first men to arrive on the Fraser secured the best places on the yellow bars, and did very well in their mining operations, but many of the late-comers, finding the river crowded, turned back to the coast in disappointment. Little camps sprang up along the river with boarding houses, saloons and stores. Flour sold for thirty-five dollars a hundred pounds, pork for one dollar a pound, beans for a dollar a pound, and salt for a dollar and twenty-five cents a pound.

By autumn all the sandbars in the lower Fraser had been staked into claims and were being worked by at least ten thousand miners and bands of Indians. Some of the miners washed as much as eight hundred dollars worth of dust and nuggets in a day, while others did not secure enough to pay their expenses. With the approach of winter, many of the less fortunate men gave up their claims, tired of hard work and scanty gains.

Although the men all carried guns in holsters, there was surprisingly little quarrelling and shooting in the mining country. The Indians, however, resented the coming of the Americans and several skirmishes broke out between the red men and white. Hearing of this, Governor James Douglas rushed inland with a group of armed men, but by the time he arrived the shooting was over. On this occasion he spoke to groups of miners and warned them once more that disturbers would be brought into court, fined or jailed.

As the sandbars of the Lower Fraser began to play out, groups of miners worked their way upstream in canoes and on horseback. Some of these pushed on and on farther into the interior; others simply disappeared and were never heard of again—lost in the swift streams, crushed by landslides, fallen over sheer cliffs to quick deaths on the rocks below. The advance guard of these miners reached Cariboo Lake almost four hundred miles inland, and there they found gold in abundance. When news of this strike spread there was another rush of miners, this time from all over the world. A group from eastern Canada made the long journey by ox-cart and river raft in four months time!

The mining fields of Cariboo brought greater difficulties in transportation for all supplies and mining equipment had to be carried from the coast. Swaying strings of sure-footed mules trudged over the rough mountain trails carrying boxes, bags, and packs on their backs, but this was a slow and costly method of bringing all the materials that were needed in the camps. It is not surprising that boots sold for fifty dollars a pair and flour for three hundred dollars a barrel.

Someone had the bright idea that if camels were used, larger loads could be moved over trails more rapidly. But when the poor animals were secured, they went lame in the mountains. Horses and mules stampeded from the strange beasts. The plan was a dismal failure.

It soon became clear that if the rich gold fields of the Cariboo were to be developed properly a good road must be

The miners washed sand and gravel from the stream beds in round metal pans. When the dirt was floated away, the men looked eagerly into the pans for signs of gold dust and nuggets.

built from the Fraser River to the mining camps. James Douglas saw the wisdom of the plan, and during the years 1862 to 1865 he built the famous Cariboo Trail, eighteen feet wide and three hundred and eighty miles long. It wound its way across wooden bridges, over deep canyons and hung dizzily to the sides of sheer rock walls that fell hundreds of feet to frothing streams below.

The coming of the Cariboo Trail changed the mining country and brought better conditions to the busy camps. Oxen drawing supply wagons and long lines of mules carried tons of food and mining equipment to Cariboo. Stage coaches flying along the road carried passengers to and from the Fraser in four days. Inns appeared along the trail, serving meals and providing rooms for the travellers that rode the painted stages.

Mining in the Cariboo country was an uncertain business, for no miner knew when his claims would cease to produce the precious metal. Some gold was found on the surface in the form of dust and nuggets, other gold was found deep in the clay after digging shafts. Miners pushed up the creeks flowing into the lake and some of these found mines that were rich beyond their wildest dreams. One creek alone gave up one hundred thousand dollars worth of gold in three weeks. Between the years 1859 and 1871, the Cariboo yielded twenty-five million dollars' worth of gold!

As in California, the surface gold was gradually picked up and the miners began to wander away. In 1863 there were twenty thousand miners in the Cariboo and eight years later less than five thousand remained. What gold was left lay deep in the earth and rocks and could be removed only by mining companies with expensive machinery.

Although the glory of the rush was over, the great movement of men had served to found the colony of British Columbia which became a part of Canada in 1871 and was joined to the east a few years later by the Canadian Pacific Railway.

James Douglas, the courageous Governor of gold rush days, is known as "The Father of British Columbia."

31   THE TRAIL OF '98

As early as the 1840's men of the Hudson's Bay Company found gold near the source of the Yukon River, and a few years later Russian traders picked up dust and nuggets a short distance upstream from the mouth. In 1867, the United States bought Alaska from Russia and American prospectors began to take an interest in the mining possibilities of the land. It was not until 1894, however, that a rich strike was made on the Klondike, a branch of the Yukon, within Canadian territory. Realizing that the third great gold rush of North American history was about to begin, the Canadian Government ordered the Mounted Police to set up posts and make preparation for the gold-hungry prospectors.

In 1897-1898 came the full force of the rush as thirty thousand miners from all over the world flooded the gold country. Up the Yukon River they came by steamboat, seventeen hundred miles from the Alaskan coast . . . up they came from Skagway on the Alaskan Panhandle, over the Chilkoot and White Passes, plodding through the snows, riding dog teams . . . down the rapids and through the canyons in rafts, boats and canoes . . . on and on to Dawson that sprawled across the muddy banks where the Klondike met the Yukon.

It was a swifter, bigger and more exciting affair than any gold rush the world had yet seen. The hardships were much greater and more terrifying than those faced by the miners of California and the Fraser, for here were blizzards, killing cold, endless drifts, snowslides, swift torrents and boiling rapids.

Mounted Police guarded all the passes, collected customs duties, turned back suspected criminals, and warned new-comers of the dangers to be met on the trails. At White Horse Rapids on the Yukon a police officer, Superintendent Steele, faced a group of newly arrived Americans, many of them from homes, stores, factories in faraway cities, their faces white and their hands soft.

He spoke in a crisp, business-like manner—"There are many of your countrymen who have said that the Mounted Police make the laws as they go along, and I am going to do so now for your own good, therefore the directions that I am going to give shall be carried out strictly . . . Corporal Dixon, who thoroughly understands this work, will be in charge here, responsible to me for the proper management of the Canyon and the White Horse Rapids. No women or children will be taken in the boats. If they are strong enough to come to the Klondike, they can walk the five miles of the bank to the foot of the White Horse and there is no danger for them here. No boat will be permitted to go through the Canyon until the corporal is satisfied that it has free board to enable it to ride the rapids in safety. No boat will be allowed to pass with human beings in it unless it is steered by competent men, and of that the corporal will be the judge."

In the spring of '98 the first wave of the rush struck the little centre of Dawson, as barges, flatboats, scows and canoes rushed down river with their crews of excited miners. This strange collection of river craft tied up along the river front until Dawson took on the appearance of a "Chinese city." Businesses sprang up like mushrooms: a daily newspaper, *The Nugget*,

Dragging heavy loads, miners made their way over mountain passes to the gold fields of the Yukon. Sometimes small sails were used to ease the burden.

started printing in a tent and soon afterwards two weekly papers, *The Midnight Sun* and the *Dawson Miner,* put in their appearance. Shops and stores opened daily: real estate agents, mining brokers, lawyers, doctors, a flower shop, a fruit store, a beauty parlour, a drygoods store, a shoeshine parlour, four drug stores and at least fifteen saloons. Women in long dresses walked daintily about the streets, boys sold newspapers, packs of dogs barked and scampered along the roadways.

Prices of food and supplies leaped to alarming heights: nails were twenty-eight dollars a pound, brooms sold for fourteen dollars each. A lonesome cow brought in on a sailboat produced milk which went at sixty dollars a gallon.

In spite of the bustle, the noise, the eagerness, the rivalry of the gold rush, it was one of the most orderly in history, for the Royal Canadian Mounted Police kept a firm hand on the miners and took swift action when Canadian laws were broken. Few hardened criminals entered the Yukon, so that gambling and gun fighting had no chance to become established. Law courts were set up and hundreds of cases were tried before judges and police officials—cases of dog stealing, drunkenness, disorderly conduct, swearing, idleness and robbery. Men who behaved like hoodlums in Alaska became very tame persons as they crossed the border into Canadian land.

News of the gold strikes along the Klondike and the little creeks of the region seeped into Dawson, causing flurries of excitement among the men of the tents and shacks. A pack-train of fifteen mules swayed down the street, each mule carrying a treasure load of twenty thousand dollars worth of gold. Miners grew rich in a few weeks, while thousands of

THE TRAIL OF '98

others made less than wages as they swung their picks and shovels. Gold was found in the most unexpected places, so that men who had never seen a mining field before made the best discoveries. "Gold is where you find it," became a popular saying among the miners.

Among the men who came to the Klondike were such hardy characters as the now legendary Klondike Mike Mahoney, who washed one hundred and sixty-five thousand dollars worth of gold in three months, travelled amazing distances, carried a piano over the Chilkoot Pass, and with a dog team moved the body of a dead judge four hundred miles through snow-covered mountains.

By the spring of 1899 the peak of the gold rush was passed and weary miners began working their way back over the dangerous trails to the coast. Big mining companies with dredges and drills took over the mining operations, pushing below the surface to the gold veins.

The trail of '98, however, left lasting results for steamers plied the Yukon River and a railway pushed northward from Skagway to White Horse, linking the coast with the headwaters of the stream, and foreshadowing the modern, prosperous communities that now lie in the northwest.

VI

32   VIRGINIA

Nearly a hundred years after Spain was established in the West Indies, England began setting up colonies on the eastern shores of America. In time there were thirteen colonies which spread along the coast from Nova Scotia to Florida. Settlement began in the days of Queen Elizabeth I when Sir Walter Raleigh made three attempts to colonize a land he called Virginia in honour of the Queen. While these attempts were failures, they did cause more interest in the New World and introduced Englishmen to the custom of smoking tobacco. Raleigh's work was not in vain, for others of his countrymen established a permanent colony in Virginia just one year before Champlain founded Quebec.

It was May, 1607. Captain John Smith stood firmly and calmly among a crowd of pale, travel-worn settlers on the deck of an English ship off the coast of America. Nearby two other vessels rode the low waves, their sails round and full in the brisk breeze.

"There lies Virginia," cried John Smith, "the land where we shall dwell, and we shall live in happiness or die in misery."

"Don't be so gloomy, John," complained an English gentleman. "Virginia is a land of good soil, a land of pleasant climate, a land of forests, a land of plenty. We shall all prosper on gold and tobacco!"

John Smith chuckled, but the tone of his voice was still serious. "I hope you are right, sir. But I believe that in America there are still such things as long winters and savage Indians. We may yet see the day when we regret leaving our homes in Old England."

"Nonsense!" scoffed the gentleman. "Even now I can see my plantation lying neat and green in the warm sunshine."

Both John Smith and the gentleman were partly correct in their prophecies, for the Colony of Virginia was to see days of misery and times of wonderful prosperity.

Near the mouth of the James River, on a swampy peninsula the hundred settlers founded the settlement of Jamestown which they named in honour of their King. Soldiers with ready muskets watched the forest for approaching Indians, as axes twinkled in the spring sunlight. A fort went up, then a church and a storehouse, forming a hopeful prospect for the settlers.

Knowing the stories of the treasures found by the Spaniards in Mexico, many of the men hoped to find gold on the shores of Virginia. When glittering stones were found along the river, a great thrill ran among the men, who dropped their tasks and scrambled to dig among the rocks. Quantities of the mineral were sent back to England in the ships, but there was no treasure in the cargoes: the glittering stones were but iron pyrites or "fool's gold."

So much valuable time was lost in the search for gold that other and more important duties were neglected. The seeds brought from England for planting were left in bags and boxes when they might have been sown in the rich soil of the new land. A good crop that first season would have prevented later suffering, but the men were too excited to think of that.

After the ships left for home, the colony began to suffer from famine and disease. The location of Jamestown in a swamp area had been a serious mistake, for mosquitoes spread

When Virginia became prosperous, shiploads of young women were sent from England to become wives of the men in the colony. Here we see a group of young women ready to leave from England.

malaria fever among the settlers, causing suffering and death. Men dropped by the dozens. Fever, other diseases and lack of food caused such havoc that only forty of the one hundred colonists were left alive when the ships came back the following January.

The arrival of the vessels with more men and some food brought little relief to the settlement, for conditions remained as miserable as ever. That the colony survived at all is due, probably, to the gallant efforts of one strong man, Captain John Smith, the hero of early Virginia. He kept the men at work, cutting trees, building homes and breaking up land for planting. No peace was given the lazy men of Jamestown, for John Smith ordered that those who did no work would get no food.

Those settlers who were not used to hard work grumbled as they dug with shovels and chopped with axes. Blisters rose on soft hands, and muscles ached with toil.

To ease the suffering, John Smith bought food from the Indians and hurried it back to the starving men at Jamestown. His travels were not without danger, for on one occasion he was captured by Indians who tied him up and coolly prepared to kill him. While steeling himself for the thrusts of knives and the blows of tomahawks, the captive was amazed to see an Indian girl, Pocahontas, run forward to protect him. With tears in her eyes she begged her father, the chief, to spare the life of the white man. The chief, just as startled as Smith had been, ordered his warriors to release John Smith and to escort him back to the settlement. Pocahontas, an attractive girl, later married John Rolfe, an Englishman, who was to become an important man in the history of Virginia.

The dreary life of the colony dragged on from one misery to another. In 1609 more settlers arrived and conditions appeared brighter, but this did not last for long. Famine, disease and Indian attacks brought the settlement almost to the stage of destruction. Of the nine hundred settlers brought into the colony during its first three years of life, only one hundred and fifty remained alive!

But instead of dying out entirely, the English in Virginia became stronger and stronger, as Jamestown was rebuilt, the Indians driven back and two new forts built at the mouth of the river. More land was cleared for the growing of crops and farm animals were brought in from England. John Rolfe, the settler who had married Pocahontas, grew the first crop of tobacco and started Virginia on the road to prosperity. Group after group of settlers appeared and these formed new settlements some distance from Jamestown.

Tobacco became the most important product of the colony

and as the years passed, large cargoes made their way back to the Old Country where they were sold at high prices. In 1619 new workers were found for the tobacco fields when a Dutch ship put in at the harbour and sold twenty negro slaves to willing English buyers. That was the beginning of slavery in Virginia, and for two centuries many a slave ship sailed from Africa to the land of tobacco.

Up until this time there had been few women in Virginia, but as life became easier in the settlements, shiploads of unmarried women were sent out from England. The men of the colony soon selected their brides and gladly gave up one hundred and twenty pounds of first grade tobacco each in payment of the ladies' ocean passage.

Some Englishmen with large land grants began to establish the famous plantations which were worked by hundreds of negro slaves. The clearing of land for this purpose, however, angered the Indians who attacked outlying settlements, killing between three and four hundred persons. The white men, furious with this slaughter, swept through the Indian country at harvest time burning the corn and almost wiping out the Indians living along the lower reaches of the James and York Rivers.

Farms and plantations continued to spread across Virginia and the number of people increased by hundreds. By 1635, twenty-eight years after the founding of Jamestown, there were five thousand persons living in the colony.

Although Captain John Smith had long since left America, the courage and determination he had shown in the early struggles of the colony were still felt in the prosperous land of Virginia.

33 THE PILGRIM FATHERS

When North America was first settled by the English, religious freedom had not yet come to the Mother Country. The Puritans, who did not agree with the laws of the established Church of England, led fearful lives, for they were persecuted by the government. King James I said that if the Puritans did not do what they were told, he would harry them out of the land.

A Puritan minister, John Robinson, and an elder, William Brewster, met on a street in the town of Scrooby, Nottinghamshire. They stopped, looked around to see that no one was listening, and then began a whispered conversation.

"William," asked the minister, "is all in readiness for our flight to Amsterdam?"

"Aye, we're ready, sir. Our people cannot stand this fear and terror any longer, but it does tear at the heart strings to leave Old England. If only we could worship as we desire in this, our land of birth!"

John Robinson sighed. "I know, William, it is hard to break the ties of blood and race, but to serve God we must get away where we can set up our church in peace and freedom."

After some difficulties the Puritans, who now became the Pilgrim Fathers, left England and sailed to Holland where they set up homes and a church. Although they were able to worship, they were not entirely happy in their new location, for they had to work hard for a poor living and they felt that they were being absorbed into Dutch life. They longed for a home where they could have their own church and still live as Englishmen. When they heard of the Colony of Virginia, they were eager to sail to the New World and establish a settlement of their own. Here was the answer to their prayers!

As quickly as they could they made arrangements for leaving Europe, buying one boat the *Speedwell,* and hiring a second, the *Mayflower.* They were fortunate enough to secure a land grant from the Virginia Company, and better still, the King agreed not to interfere with their life in America. The brave expedition set out; the *Speedwell* proved to be unseaworthy and the whole company had to be placed in the *Mayflower.* The minister, John Robinson, remained in Holland and the doughty old William Brewster took command.

The *Mayflower* with one hundred and two people aboard sailed for weeks across the Atlantic, driven by gales until the Captain of the vessel lost his reckoning. Well north of Virginia, they first sighted land at Cape Cod—a shore on which they had no permission to settle. They attempted to sail southward to the land which had been granted to them, but finally turned back and found refuge in the harbour nestled in the crook of Cape Cod.

They decided to remain where they were and secure a land holding at a later time. Before going ashore the Pilgrim Fathers assembled in the ship and all the men signed a paper —the famous *Mayflower* Compact by which they agreed to form their own government and obey the laws of their elected officers.

Men were sent ashore to explore the land and these found the country cold and bleak, snow on the ground and a brisk wind whipping seaspray over their clothing until it froze like "coats of iron." Later a small party under Captain Miles Standish discovered Plymouth harbour, and there on December 1620, the Pilgrims landed and fell on their knees

THE THIRTEEN COLONIES

to thank God for bringing them across a "vast and furious" ocean.

Within a few days axes were ringing in the forest and little cabins were rising in a clearing. That winter, cold, disease and lack of food took a toll of forty lives and among the dead was the first governor, John Carver. William Bradford was elected in his place, and he lived to be governor for the next thirty-one years.

Few Indians lived in the region of Plymouth, as some years before hundreds of them had died in a great epidemic. However, in March, 1621, a lone Indian walked calmly into the settlement and astonished the Puritans by shouting, "Welcome, Englishmen!" This friendly visitor had picked up a few English words from fishermen working along the coast of Maine, and he was now taking great delight in showing off his knowledge. He then disappeared and a few days later came back with a second Indian, Squanto, who, oddly enough, spoke English too. The newcomer proved a most valuable friend to the settlers, for he taught them the secrets of fishing, hunting and planting corn with dead fish for fertilizer. Some years afterward, at the time of his death Squanto begged that the Puritans would pray that he be sent to the white man's Heaven. Squanto's friendship proved important in another way, for it led to a peace treaty with his tribe, a treaty which was kept faithfully for the next fifty years.

In the beginning, all land was worked in common and the crops produced were distributed among the families. This plan, while it appeared to be a wise one, did not operate successfully, as a few lazy men in the settlement let the others do most of the work. This, as might be expected, caused unhappiness and discontentment, and finally it was agreed that each man would till his own land. Conditions became more prosperous and the colony grew slowly. At the end of twelve years about three hundred Puritans were settled near Plymouth.

They managed to secure rights to the land on which they lived, although it took them seven years to make full payment to the London merchants.

The Puritan colonists were amazed one day when a lone Indian walked into their settlement, and shouted "Welcome Englishmen!" Notice the long dresses, the bonnets of the women, and the broad hat worn by the man.

The Puritans kept their democratic form of rule on which they had agreed in the *Mayflower* Compact. During the first sixteen years Governor Bradford presided over the "town meeting," which was attended by all the men of the colony.

After that, the settlement became too large for such an assembly and representatives were elected to look after the affairs of government.

Although the Pilgrim Fathers may have been a grim, strict people who appeared to get little enjoyment from life, they were, at the same time, a sturdy, dauntless God-fearing group who planted a solid British colony in America and laid the foundations for the present State of Massachusetts.

34 NEW AMSTERDAM

We often speak of the Thirteen English Colonies that stretched along the Atlantic coast of America. Did you know that one of them, New York, was first founded by the Dutch?

On a clear bright day in September, 1609, a small vessel of the Dutch East India Company sailed into what is now the harbour of New York and skirted the unfamiliar shores.

On board the ship an officer approached the English Captain, Henry Hudson, drew himself up smartly and reported, "There is a waterway leading northward to the interior, sir."

"Very good," exclaimed Hudson, "have the helmsman change course and enter it."

The *Half Moon* shifted a few degrees to the north and thrust her wooden bow into the current, moving slowly up the broad waterway. As the hours and days passed, Hudson watched the shores, admiring the thick forests and the purple ridges of the Catskill Mountains. Tides rose and fell in the passage, giving the English captain hope that here was a new and important discovery. Like dozens of other seamen before him, Hudson dreamed of finding the North West Passage to the Pacific.

On and on went the *Half Moon* until she reached a point near the spot where the city of Albany now stands. There, when the passage narrowed and the salt water turned to fresh, Hudson realized that he had been sailing a river which could not possibly take him to a western sea. Disappointed, he turned back on the river we now call the Hudson, and then sailed for Holland.

Although the Dutch East India Company considered Hudson's voyage a failure, it was in reality a great success, for it led to very important events: Indian furs brought back on the *Half Moon* excited a number of Dutch merchants who organized the Dutch West India Company and sent trading expeditions to the Hudson River. A post called Fort Orange was built at Albany and another, Fort Amsterdam, was set up on Manhattan Island at the mouth of the river. This island where New York City now stands, was bought from the Indians with trade goods worth about twenty-four dollars—today a single building lot on Broadway would cost ten thousand times as much!

A settlement, known as New Amsterdam, grew up about the trading post on Manhattan Island, but its growth was slow. Dissatisfied with this situation, the Dutch West India Company began to offer large land holdings to important Dutchmen who could bring at least fifty settlers to the colony. These new landowners, or *patroons*, were granted estates, each of which extended for sixteen miles along the shores of the Hudson.

The *patroons* lived like noblemen in big homes which were well decorated and filled with fine furniture from Europe. They governed their huge estates and controlled the lives of the poor people who worked the land. Little better off than servants, these unfortunates were forced to sell their crops to the *patroon* and to grind their grain at his mill. On rent day a procession of farmers and loaded wagons made their way to the owner's home to pay their land dues for the year, and there they feasted, danced and sang for a few short hours. The *patroons* became a wealthy and powerful group of families which were destined to become famous in American history.

People who wished to build homes and work their own land did not come to the Dutch colony at first, but in later years when land was made free there was a rush of settlers from Europe, Maine, Massachusetts, Maryland and Virginia.

The settlers along the Hudson had never been allowed to rule themselves as were the people of the British colonies. They became discontented, demanding more freedom and a voice in government, but very few improvements were made by the Dutch West India Company.

In 1664 King Charles II of England very generously gave his brother, the Duke of York, all the land lying between Connecticut and the Delaware River. The fact that the Dutch occupied the valley of the Hudson did not bother the King in the least. That same year a small fleet of British naval vessels sailed from England with five hundred seasoned troops aboard, and more militia men were picked up in the colonies. The fleet then sailed on to New Amsterdam and demanded the surrender of the fort.

When the English demand was received by Stuyvesant, the Dutch Governor, he roared in rage, tearing up the paper and stamping his wooden leg on the floor. "I had rather," he shouted, "be carried a corpse to my grave than surrender the city!" He was eager to resist the invaders, but his people refused to fight, knowing as they did that they could do nothing against the English troops and naval cannon. So the peppery Stuyvesant was forced to surrender, and the British flag went up over New Amsterdam.

English war vessels appeared off the Dutch settlement of New Amsterdam. Here a Dutch settler runs from his mill to warn the other colonists of danger. What do we call New Amsterdam today?

The coming of the English brought surprisingly little change to the colony, for the Dutch people kept their customs, their dress and their flourishing farms along the Hudson. New Amsterdam became New York in honour of the Duke of York, and Fort Orange became Albany. In time the settlers were given a government very much like that of the other British colonies along the Atlantic coast. The steady, dependable Dutch and the hardy, adventurous English lived peacefully with each other, and together formed what is now the state of New York.

35 PENNSYLVANIA

One of the largest of the English colonies was founded by a man who gave up an important position in life to find a shelter for unfortunate people in America. Pennsylvania was established at the time that La Salle was making his famous explorations on the Mississippi.

Admiral Penn faced his son, expressions of anger and bewilderment crossing his handsome face.

"William," he snapped. "What is this I hear from Oxford about you becoming a Quaker?"

Young William Penn sat down slowly, leaned back in the chair and answered his father calmly. "That's quite true, sir. I have joined the Quakers and I confess that I am quite happy in this faith."

"Ridiculous!" snorted the admiral. "Utterly ridiculous! I had great hopes for your future; you showed such promise in riding, hunting, swordsmanship and your studies at Oxford. Now you are a Quaker! What will our friends think? What will the King think?"

William appeared to be quite unconcerned by the thought

of his friends and the monarch. "Surely, father," he said quietly, "a man has the right to worship as he wishes!"

The admiral puffed angrily and his face turned red. "Young man," he thundered, "you can worship in the Church of England without joining this ignorant rabble! Quakers indeed! I hate the sight of them with their dull dress, their stern faces and their silly 'thee's' and 'thou's.' Stiff unmannerly people they are, keeping their hats on even in the presence of nobility!"

William sighed. "We Quakers believe that every man is as good as another. I myself will not take off my hat even to Charles II!"

Although Admiral Penn quarrelled violently with his son on this occasion, he later relented, and at the time of his death he left William a large fortune.

Like the Puritans before them, the Quakers encountered difficulties with the British authorities. They refused to support the established church; they would not take their hats off to anyone; they worshipped together against the law; they spoke out against the cruel treatment of insane people and prisoners; they preached that wars were sinful and wasteful. It is not surprising that in England of that time they found themselves in courts and prisons.

The idea of founding a Quaker colony in America occurred to William Penn, and in time an opportunity to do this appeared. It happened that King Charles owed a sum of money to Admiral Penn, and after his father's death Penn asked the King to pay the debt in American land. Since King Charles was only too happy to do this, Penn received a royal grant and charter for a large tract of land stretching westward from the Delaware River. This new district came to be known as Pennsylvania, meaning "Penn's Woodland."

Settlers for the colony were soon found, for the Quakers had every faith and confidence in William Penn. During

September, 1682, he and a hundred people sailed from England abord the ship *Welcome,* and reached the Delaware River. Some distance upstream the Quakers began building Philadelphia (the City of Brotherly Love), a settlement which was to flourish in an amazing manner. The hard working Quakers little dreamed that in a few years Philadelphia was to become the most important city in the colonies and much later was to be the birthplace of a new nation. Just four years after its founding it was larger than New York which had been founded more than fifty years earlier .

Since the Quakers did not believe in war, William Penn was very anxious to make peace with the Indians of the district. In the shade of a giant elm he smoked the pipe of peace and spoke in a kindly manner to a circle of Delaware red men. The Indians were so impressed by the attitude of the Quakers that they agreed to a treaty, promising to "live in love with William Penn and his children as long as the sun and moon give light." A chieftain gave William Penn a beaded belt of wampum into which was worked the picture of an Indian and a white man holding hands in friendship. The treaty was kept faithfully during the lifetime of the Quaker leader.

Philadelphia was laid out in a neat and precise fashion, its streets running at right angles to each other like a checkerboard. Houses of frame and brick were placed in spacious lots which had gardens, lawns and shade trees. On Sundays the Quakers gathered in the meetinghouse, a square brick building, the interior of which was plain and unornamented. The men wore drab clothes, knee breeches, broad-brimmed hats and large white collars; the women dressed in grey dresses, white kerchiefs and wide black bonnets. The men, with their hats on, sat stiffly on one side of the meetinghouse, while the women remained on the other.

Although William Penn owned all the land in Pennsylvania

and had the right to set up any kind of government he desired, he allowed great freedom to his people. Citizens held land in their own names and they voted their representatives into the assembly of the colony.

King Charles II granted William Penn a large tract of land in America near the Delaware River. Here William Penn, dressed as a Quaker, stands before the King.

Filled with a sympathy for the poor and down-trodden, Penn invited settlers from many countries in Europe to come to Pennsylvania. Some came from Wales and France. A group of Mennonites from the Rhine Valley of Germany founded Germantown north of Philadelphia. Eighteen years after the colony was established people from Northern Ireland began arriving in America, and most of these settled in Penn's colony. These adventurous newcomers pushed into the western limits of Pennsylvania, and future generations moved across the mountains to the prairies and on toward the Pacific.

Little settlements dotted the forest with their clearings, Philadelphia expanded, schools and churches sprouted here and there. Although Pennsylvania was next to the last of the thirteen British Colonies to be founded in America, it grew more rapidly than the others and became one of the most important. William Penn, who had willingly given up wealth and high position, devoted himself unselfishly to giving poor and troubled people a haven in the New World. When he died he willed the colony to his three sons, John, Thomas and Richard, and they and their descendants held it until the days of the American Revolution.

It was in Pennsylvania that the first daily newspaper in the colonies was printed. It was here too that great citizens such as Benjamin Franklin arose and that a new nation came into being.

Thus it was that our continent became the settled community we know today. It is a far cry from the voyages of Columbus and Cartier to those of Stefansson and Henry Larsen, but each added something to man's knowledge of the country. And when the explorers had gone their way, settlers followed wave on wave to build the North America of the twentieth century.

TIME-CHART

In the West

In the East

1490

Columbus reaches America
John Cabot explores the east
coast

1500

1510

Ponce de Léon in Florida

1520

Pizarro in Peru

Cortés in Mexico

1530

Cartier on the St. Lawrence

1540

De Soto reaches the
Mississippi

1550

1560

1570

Drake in the Pacific

1580

1590

1600

The French at Port Royal
The English found Virginia
Champlain founds Quebec
Henry Hudson discovers the
Hudson River

221

In the West   *In the East*

1610	
	Henry Hudson discovers Hudson Bay
	Champlain explores parts of what are now Southern Ontario and New York State
1620	
	The Pilgrim Fathers land in Plymouth
	The Dutch found New Amsterdam
1630	
1640	
1650	
1660	
	Radisson and Groseilliers reached Hudson Bay
1670	
	The Hudson's Bay Company is formed
	Marquette and Joliet explore the Mississippi
1680	
	La Salle reaches the mouth of the Mississippi
	Pennsylvania is founded by William Penn
	Daniel Du Lhut on the prairies
1690	
1700	

In the West

In the East

	1710	
	1720	
	1730	
		The prairie explorations of La Vérendrye
	1740	
Vitus Bering reaches Alaska		
	1750	
	1760	
		Canada becomes British
		Samuel Hearne follows the Coppermine River to the Arctic
	1770	
The Spanish move into California		The American Revolution
Capt. Cook on the west coast		The United States of America is formed
		Alexander Henry on the prairies
	1780	
Capt. Vancouver at Nootka Sound		The North West Company is formed
Alexander Mackenzie reaches the Arctic		
	1790	
Capt. Vancouver charts the northwest coast		
Alexander Mackenzie reaches the Pacific by land		
	1800	
Simon Fraser explores the Fraser River		
	1810	
David Thompson completes first map of the northwest		

In the West   *In the East*

	1820	
		The Hudson's Bay Company
		and the North West
		Company are united
	1830	
	1840	
Gold rush in California		
	1850	
Gold rush to the Fraser		
	1860	
United States buys Alaska from Russia		
	1870	
	1880	
	1890	
Gold rush to the Yukon		
	1900	
	1910	
Stefansson discovers new islands in the Arctic		
	1920	
	1930	
	1940	
St. Roch completes the N.W. Passage		
	1950	
		St. Roch completes voyage
		around North America

THINGS TO KNOW

ADOBE

Adobe bricks were made from clay, water and straw or hay. After being carefully kneaded and tramped by the bare feet of the natives, the mixture was poured into shallow wooden boxes, and left to dry in the sun. This old method of making bricks is still used in Mexico, Central America, South America, and other parts of the world. When adobe brick is used in walls, gateways and houses, it is often covered with a coating of plaster to protect the adobe from the weather. In dry, warm climates adobe walls will last for hundreds of years.

ANTARCTIC CIRCLE

In order to understand what is meant by the Antarctic Circle, we must think of the earth as being divided into five big regions by means of four parallels of latitude. These four imaginary lines are called: the Arctic Circle, the Tropic of Cancer, the Tropic of Capricorn, and the *Antarctic Circle*.

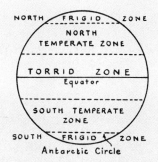

These four lines divide the earth's surface into five regions called *zones*. The five zones are called: the North Frigid Zone, the North Temperate Zone, the Torrid Zone, the South Temperate Zone and the South Frigid Zone.

The *Antarctic Circle* lies about 23 degrees from the South Pole.

ASTRONOMY

Astronomy is the oldest of all the sciences. It is the study of heavenly bodies and their relationship to each other. Astronomers can tell us how far stars are from the earth, how the planets move in great circles, how hot the sun is, how the moon reflects light, why the stars shine, how meteors burn themselves up, and many other amazing things about the worlds that lie out in space.

BARNACLES

Barnacles are tiny sea animals which swim free in the ocean when they are young. When they become adults, they attach themselves to rocks or other objects, and there they remain for the rest of their lives. The body of the adult barnacle is protected by a hard, sharp shell which has several parts.

In the days of wooden sailing ships the barnacles proved to be a great nuisance, because they attached themselves to the ships' hulls below the surface of the water. Gradually a heavy coating of barnacles was formed, causing the ships to become slow and sluggish in movement. When this happened, the ships had to be taken out of water and scraped. Finally seamen discovered that if they put a covering of copper over the hulls, the barnacles would not fasten themselves to the ships.

BARREN LANDS

The barren lands of northern Canada lie above the prairies and the forests. They are *tundra* regions too cold for the growth of grasses and trees. The soil there is usually a black muck in which grow mosses, lichens, small shrubs and flowering plants. The Barren Lands are the home of the caribou and the musk ox.

CANYON

Deep valleys with high steep sides are called canyons. These are found in regions where swift rivers wear the rocks and soil away in a very rapid manner. Perhaps the world's most famous canyon is the Grand Canyon of the Colorado River in the southwestern part of the United States. This magnificent canyon, in places, is 6,000 feet deep, and is from eight to fifteen miles wide across the top.

CARIBOU

The caribou of northern Canada is closely related to the reindeer of Lapland. It is a fairly large animal with large spreading horns and broad hoofs. In colour, it is a dark brown above and white below. Large herds of caribou make long journeys, or migrations, across the barren lands during the spring and autumn months.

DYEWOOD TREES

There are several trees in the West Indies which contain material which can be used for the making of dyes. Examples of these are the *fustic* which produces a light-yellow colour, and the *logwood* which produces a blue colour. The cutting and preparing of these trees was an important industry in the Spanish colonies.

GULF STREAM

The Gulf Stream is a warm, clear, blue current of water that flows from the Gulf of Mexico northward along the eastern coast of the United States. It is quite possible to stand on a ship, and watch the Gulf Stream flowing like a river in the waters of the ocean. After reaching the eastern coast of Canada, the current swings eastward across the Atlantic in the direction of Europe. Such countries as France, England, Scotland and Ireland have mild climates because they are affected by the warm waters of the Gulf Stream.

LATITUDE

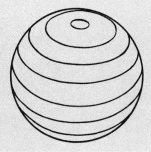

Latitude is the distance north or south of the equator. Latitude is measured in degrees. There are 90 degrees between the equator and each of the poles. Parallels of latitude are imaginary lines drawn around the earth, running in the same direction as the equator. By finding latitude, explorers were able to tell how far north or south of the equator they were.

LLAMA

The camel has a long-necked relative in the Andes Mountains of South America. This animal, which is not as large as the camel, is called the llama. It is sure-footed, strong and very hardy. Thick coarse wool covers its body. The llama can carry a load of more than one hundred pounds over steep mountain trails where neither horses nor mules could travel. Besides its value in transportation, the llama is important because it provides meat and milk. It is related to two other South American animals: the *alpaca* and the *vicuña*.

LONGITUDE

Longitude is distance east or west of the standard meridian which passes through Greenwich, England. Longitude, like latitude, is measured in degrees. Meridians of longitude are imaginary circles passing around the earth from pole to pole. When navigators were able to find both longitude and latitude by means of instruments, they could locate their exact sailing positions on maps and charts.

MALARIA

Malaria is a serious disease found in many parts of the world, although it is most frequent in hot tropical countries. For centuries it caused more illness and death than any other disease. Modern medicine has done much to reduce the danger of malaria, but even now thousands of people die each year from this disease. Those suffering from it have high fever followed by terrible chills. Malaria is spread from person to person through the bite of the *Anopheles* mosquito.

MANATEE

The manatee is a large water animal which lives in bays, rivers and lagoons, but not in the open sea. Somewhat whale-like in appearance, the manatee varies in length from eight to thirteen feet. It has two large flippers in front and a broad tail behind. This animal feeds on plants growing in shallow water. It is harmless, but is hunted frequently for the sake of its oil, hide and meat. In America, manatees are found in Florida, Mexico, Central America and South America.

NORTH MAGNETIC POLE

When we say that a compass points to the north, we mean that it points in the direction of the North Magnetic Pole. This Magnetic Pole is not in the same location as the North Pole, but lies some hundreds of miles to the south in northern Canada. The North Magnetic Pole does not remain in exactly the same place, but moves slowly from year to year. It must be remembered that there is a South Magnetic Pole as well.

NORTH POLE

The earth spins round and round just as if it were turning on a great pole thrust through its centre. There is no such pole, of course, but we often find it useful to think of an imaginary line passing through the earth. This line is called the *axis* of the earth. The point where the axis comes out at the top we call the North Pole. The point where the axis comes out at the bottom we call the South Pole.

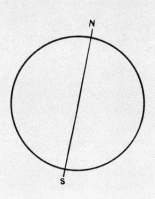

PASS

A pass is a passage through a range of mountains. Many such natural passes have been formed by swift rivers pushing their way to the sea. Roads, highways, and railways usually are constructed through passes in mountainous country.

PASSENGER PIGEON

Great numbers of wild pigeons were seen by the early explorers of North America. These birds were the famous passenger pigeons which lived in millions throughout the central parts of this continent. Flying in huge flocks, they sometimes darkened the sky for hours at a time. When the settlers came, the birds were killed in great numbers for food. Finally only a few remained, and the last passenger pigeon died in captivity in 1914.

PENINSULA

A peninsula is a piece of land very nearly surrounded by water, and connected to a larger body of land.

THE PLAGUE

Bubonic plague, or the Black Death, is a disease which has caused much suffering and death through the course of world history. More than 25 million people died in Europe in an epidemic during the fourteenth century. Although the plague is no longer a great menace, it still appears from time to time. The disease attacks suddenly, causing headaches, fever, inflamed eyes, enlarged tongue, swollen glands, and too often ends in death. During the years 1664 and 1665, the Great Plague struck London, England, killing thousands of people and terrifying everyone.

PORTAGE

Very often on a canoe trip it is necessary to carry canoes and supplies from one lake to another lake, or from one river to another river. These short overland trips are called portages.

PRAIRIES

When the first explorers found their way to the centre of North America, they found vast level plains covered with long grasses. These lands were the prairies, the home of the Indian, the buffalo, the antelope and the coyote. Later, when settlers pushed into the west, the rich soil of the prairies was ploughed and grain was sown. Today the prairies of Canada and the United States make up one of the great wheat growing areas of the world. While the land is still fertile, it sometimes becomes so dry that the soil is blown away by strong winds.

PTARMIGAN

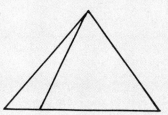

The ptarmigan is a northern bird which belongs to the same family as the grouse and the partridge. It changes from brown to white at the beginning of each winter. Oddly enough, it seeks shelter from the cold by diving into snow drifts. Indians and Eskimos hunt the ptarmigan for food.

PYRAMID

The Egyptians made great stone buildings called pyramids. These were square at the bottom, but sloped from all sides to a peak at the top. The pyramids had rooms and galleries inside them, and below the level of the ground. Each pyramid was a monument erected in honour of some very important person. Thousands of men worked for years during the building of the largest pyramids.

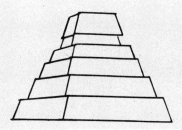

The Aztec Indians constructed pyramids too, although these were somewhat different in shape. Whereas the Egyptian pyramids tapered to a peak at the top, the Aztec pyramids were surmounted by platforms, altars and temples.

SCURVY

The disease of scurvy is caused by a lack of vitamin C in a diet. People who have this disease suffer from swollen gums, loosening teeth, ugly red spots on their skins and a feeling of great weakness. Through the course of history thousands of sailors, traders, soldiers and explorers died from scurvy because they lived on salted pork and sea biscuits during long voyages. When people have fresh meat, fruits and vegetables to eat, there is no danger from scurvy.

SEA-COW

The sea-cow is a large water animal, brown in colour, which sometimes reaches a length of twenty-five feet. It has a small head, two front flippers and a wide flat tail. It belongs to the same family as the manatee. At the time of Vitus Bering, large numbers of sea-cows lived along the coasts of Siberia and Alaska in the region of Bering Strait. Later, Russian traders killed so many of them that they almost disappeared from those waters.

SEA-OTTER

Along the coast of the north Pacific there lived a remarkable water animal, about four feet in length, which was known as the sea-otter. Centuries ago there lived countless thousands of these creatures, but the Indians killed so many of them for trading purposes, that today they are among the rarest animals in the world. The rich grey-brown fur of the sea-otter is the most valuable known to man. Recently three of these otters were flown from the Aleutian Islands to the United States to take part in a television programme. They were described as "looking like little old men, and acting like very grumpy ones."

SURVEYING

Surveying is the science of measuring and recording areas of land and water. Surveyors are interested in measuring length and width, setting up boundaries, finding the height of hills and the depth of valleys. Early surveyors drew the boundary lines of our properties, our townships, our counties and our countries. Today many surveyors are used to lay out railroads, highways, canals, tunnels, timber limits, and mining properties.

TABOO OR TABU

The idea of taboo was connected with the religion of the Polynesian people living in the South Pacific. When something was placed under taboo, no native might touch it, or, in some cases, even look at it. Things, persons, places were taboo because they were thought to be unclean, dangerous, important or even sacred. Some things were always taboo, but native priests could set up taboos for a short time only, if they wished to do so. For example, if certain waters were declared taboo, natives could not swim, paddle or fish there. Sometimes white men broke taboos without knowing what they were doing. This, of course, caused bad feelings between the explorers and the Polynesians. Taboos of various kinds have existed among native peoples in other parts of the world as well.

TEPEE

The Indians of the plains lived in leather tents called tepees, or tipis. To make a tepee, a number of animal skins were sewn together to form a large semi-circle. This was stretched over a group of poles arranged in a circle at the bottom, and tied together in a bunch at the top. The tepee was ventilated from above by means of two smoke-flaps which could be moved about with poles to suit the direction of the wind. During stormy weather, the smoke-flaps could be closed, like a coat collar, to keep out rain and snow. A small doorway in the front of the tepee was covered by a skin door which was almost round in shape. These tents were often decorated with colourful paintings of Indians, horses, wild animals, birds, stars, the moon, and simple designs. One of the chief advantages of the tepee was that it could be taken down easily, and moved to another camping place. See the illustration on page 69.

TLACHTLI

The Aztecs were very fond of games and sports. One of their favourite games was a kind of ball game called tlachtli. In this game the players tried to knock a rubber ball through a stone ring which was attached in a vertical position to a high wall. The game was very difficult to play because the players could not use their hands, feet, or heads. They had to hit the ball with their hips.

TRAVOIS

You may think of a travois as an Indian wagon which had no wheels. It was made of several long poles which trailed behind a horse or a dog. The free ends of the poles simply dragged along the ground. Several cross bars kept the poles from spreading too far apart. To the travois were tied: tepees, bundles, weapons, and other articles belonging to the Indian families.

THINGS TO DO

The Dawn of American Discovery
[1 – 6]

1. Using a map of Asia trace a route similar to those taken by the old camel caravans that travelled from China across Afghanistan, over the Euphrates River to Constantinople.

2. On a map of Europe find: England, Spain, France, Portugal, Italy and Holland.

3. How did the Crusades hasten the re-discovery of America in 1492?

4. In what country was the seaman's compass invented?

5. When did the Norsemen reach America?

6. Tell how a geographer's error gave the New World its name of America.

The Cities of Gold
[7 – 46]

1. On a map of North America find: The West Indies, the Caribbean Sea, Cuba, Haiti, Jamaica, Panama, Mexico, Mexico City, Vera Cruz, Florida, Mississippi River.

2. Under what circumstances did Florida receive its name?

3. Of what importance were the voyages of Ponce de Leon?

4. Why did the Aztec people build the Floating Gardens?

5. Paint a picture to show the Floating Gardens, canals and Indian canoes.

6. The Aztecs had no written language, but they did keep records. How did they manage to do this?

7. Why did Hernando Cortés wish to conquer the Empire of the Aztecs?

8. What was the fate of the Emperor Montezuma?

9. Why was it that a small army of Spaniards was able to overrun Mexico?

10. What is the oldest permanent city in the Americas?

11. What domestic animals did the Incas possess?

12. What modern countries of South America were included in the Inca Empire?

13. Of what materials did the Incas build their highways?

14. In what way was the stonework of the Incas so remarkable?

15. Why was it that a tiny Spanish army was able to conquer the Inca Empire?

16. Refer to your Time-Chart and see if Pizarro reached Peru before or after Champlain came to the St. Lawrence.

17. Match the names of men listed below with the facts listed to the right:

Cortés   Conquest of Peru
De Leon   Inca Ruler
Montezuma   Exploration in Florida
Pizarro   Emperor of the Aztecs
Atahualpa   Conquest of Mexico
De Soto   Discovery of the Mississippi

Quest for the Orient
[47 – 92]

1. Using a map of Canada find: Newfoundland, Strait of Belle Isle, Anticosti Island, Gaspé, New Brunswick, Chaleur Bay, Prince Edward Island, Annapolis Royal, Quebec, Three Rivers, Montreal, Ottawa River, Georgian Bay, Bay of Quinte, Sault Ste. Marie.

2. Using a map of United States find: Lake Champlain, Mackinac, Green Bay, Mississippi River, Ohio River, Wisconsin River, Missouri River, Arkansas River, Louisiana, New Orleans.

3. What French people came to America before Jacques Cartier?

4. Draw a picture to illustrate the scene where Jacques Cartier raised the wooden cross on Gaspé and claimed the land for France.

5. Why were the three voyages of Cartier important?

6. Draw a map showing the important explorations of Samuel de Champlain.

7. Why did Champlain's colony at Quebec grow so slowly?

8. Pretend that you are Champlain. Describe your experiences in the battle of 1615 with the Iroquois.

9. For what purpose did Champlain use an astrolabe?

10. Why did England give Quebec back to France in 1632?

11. Why were Joliet and Marquette interested in the Mississippi River?

12. Using a map of United States trace the route taken by Joliet and Marquette from Mackinac to the mouth of the Arkansas River.

13. What was so remarkable about La Salle's vessel, *Griffon?*

14. Why do we say that La Salle's career was clouded by misfortune?

15. What ambitious plan did La Salle have for the Mississippi Valley?

16. What two French bushrangers played an important part in the founding of the Hudson's Bay Company?

17. Why did Radisson disagree with the Governor of New France?

18. What was the aim of Henry Hudson's voyages in the North?

19. Pretend that you are Henry Hudson. Describe the mutiny aboard the *Discovery.*

20. Match the names of the men on the left with the facts on the right:

(a) Cartier   Mississippi River
     Champlain   Hudson's Bay Company
     Radisson   St. Malo
     Groseilliers   Quebec
     Joliet   Brother-in-law of Radisson

(b) Marquette   The *Discovery*
     La Salle   St. Ignace
     Tonti   Louisiana
     Hudson   The Silver Hand
     Donnacona   Stadacona

Fur Traders and Bushrangers
[93 – 127]

1. Using a map of Canada find: Lake Nipigon, Fort William, Lake of the Woods, Winnipeg, Portage La Prairie, Lake Manitoba, Churchill, Coppermine River, Lake Athabaska.

2. Who was known as the "King of the Coureurs de Bois"?

3. Look up your Time-Chart and see if La Vérendrye's explorations came before or after the founding of the Hudson's Bay Company.

4. What was the chief purpose of La Vérendrye's explorations?

5. Where did the La Vérendryes first see Indian horses?

6. Why were the buffalo so important to the Indians of the prairies?

7. Draw a picture to illustrate a camp of the Plains Indians.

8. How was pemmican made?

9. For what purpose did Samuel Hearne make his first journey to the Arctic Ocean?

10. Tell what contributions Samuel Hearne made, other than those of exploration.

11. How did the capture of Quebec by the English, in 1759, affect the western fur trade?

12. Why did the Nor' Westers find it necessary to join together and form the North West Company?

13. Pretend that you are a fur trader. Write a description of Grand Portage as it was in the days of the Nor' Westers.

14. How did the North West Company and the Hudson's Bay Company finally settle their differences?

15. Fill in the blanks:

    (a) La Vérendrye's son, ..., was ambushed by Sioux Indians.

    (b) .... was an officer in the French King's guard.

    (c) .... was a faithful Indian guide to Samuel Hearne.

(d) The big freight canoes came from Montreal, and met the light western canoes at .... on Lake Superior.

(e) Alexander Henry was almost killed by hostile Indians at ....

Northwest and North
[128 – 164]

1. On maps of Asia and North America find: Russia, Siberia, Peninsula of Kamchatka, Bering Strait, Bering Sea, Alaska, Lake Athabaska, Athabaska River, Peace River, Slave River, Great Slave Lake, Mackenzie River, Great Bear Lake, Fraser River, Bella Coola River, Columbia River, Vancouver Island, Yukon, Beaufort Sea.

2. What was so unusual about the journeys of Vitus Bering?

3. What was the most important result of the Bering voyages?

4. Trace on a map the two journeys made by Alexander Mackenzie.

5. Pretend that you are one of Mackenzie's men. Describe the scene of Mackenzie writing the message on the rock.

6. What geographical error did Simon Fraser make during his explorations on the west coast?

7. Why were the Nor' Westers so anxious to reach the Pacific?

8. What did David Thompson find at the mouth of the Columbia River?

9. What important map did David Thompson draw after his explorations were completed?

10. What did Stefansson accomplish during five years in the Arctic?

11. Why was the *St. Roch* particularly well suited for Arctic sailing?

12. How long did it take the *St. Roch* to sail from Vancouver to Halifax?

13. What explorer sailed the North West Passage first?

14. What explorer reached the North Pole first?

15. Select the proper word from the list at the right:

(a) On his second voyage Bering reached ....
California
Alaska
South America

(b) The Columbia River was explored by ....
Fraser
Mackenzie
Thompson

(c) Simon Fraser was an employee of ....
Hudson's Bay Company
North West Company
Pacific Fur Company

(d) Stefansson was born in ....
Canada
United States
Iceland

(e) The first ship to sail around North America was ....
St. Roch
Discovery
Half Moon

(f) The captain of the St. Roch was ....
Franklin
Peary
Larsen

Romance of the Pacific Coast
[165 – 199]

1. Using a map of North America find: Vancouver Island, California, San Francisco, Victoria, Fraser River, Alaska, Yukon River, Klondike River, Dawson.

2. Why did Francis Drake sail into the Pacific Ocean?

3. What did Drake have to say about a passage leading through America from Pacific to Atlantic?

4. Tell why the Spaniards moved north from Mexico into California.

5. What was Captain James Cook looking for when he sailed to Nootka Sound?

6. What business sent Captain George Vancouver to Nootka Sound?

7. Describe the meeting between Vancouver and Don Quadra.

8. How was the problem of Nootka territory finally solved?

9. Tell how gold was first discovered in California.

10. Draw a picture of the Forty-Niners crossing the prairies on the way to the gold fields.

11. How did James Douglas control the miners during the gold rush to the Fraser?

12. Why was it necessary to build the Cariboo Trail?

13. Why was the gold rush to the Yukon comparatively free from lawlessness and crime?

14. Describe Dawson City as it was in 1898.

15. How did the miners get from the Pacific coast into the Klondike gold fields?

16. Match the names of men on the left with facts listed on the right:

Drake	Charted west coast
Cook	Spanish representative
Quadra	*Golden Hind*
Vancouver	Killed in Sandwich Islands
Meares	Fort at Nootka Sound
Douglas	Governor

Cabins in the Wilderness
[201 – 220]

1. Using a map of the United States find: Maine, New Hampshire, Vermont, Massachusetts, Rhode Island, Connecticut, New York, Pennsylvania, Maryland, Virginia, North Carolina, South Carolina, Georgia.

2. Refer to your Time-Chart, and answer the following questions:

   (a) Was Virginia founded before or after Quebec?

   (b) Did the Pilgrim Fathers land at Plymouth before the French were at Port Royal?

(c) Do you think Samuel de Champlain was still living when the Dutch founded New Amsterdam?

(d) Did Canada become British before or after the American Revolution?

3. In what ways did Captain John Smith help the colony of Virginia to survive during its early period?

4. Who was the first white man to grow tobacco in Virginia?

5. When did the first negro slaves appear in Virginia?

6. Explain why the Pilgrim Fathers left England.

7. In what year did the Pilgrims land at Plymouth?

8. Draw a picture to illustrate the scene of Squanto teaching the Puritans to plant corn.

9. Explain what connection Henry Hudson had with the founding of New Amsterdam.

10. Who were the *patroons*?

11. What name did the English give to New Amsterdam?

12. What does the name Pennsylvania mean?

13. Describe the dress worn by the Quaker men and women.

14. What city was known as the "City of Brotherly Love"?

15. Match the names of men on the left with places listed on the right:

John Smith	Pennsylvania
William Brewster	Virginia
Governor Stuyvesant	New Amsterdam
William Penn	Plymouth

16. Match the names of men on the left with the names of ships listed on the right:

Henry Hudson	*Mayflower*
Miles Standish	*Half Moon*
William Penn	*Welcome*

INDEX

243

SOME BOOKS TO READ

*Archer, A. B., *Exploration and Discovery*, Cambridge

*Baker, J. N. L., *A History of Geographical Discovery and Exploration*, Harrap

Boog-Watson and Carruthers, *Beyond the Sunset*, Oxford

Bowden et al, *The Day before Yesterday In America*, Macmillan

Brendon, J. A., *Great Navigators and Discoverers*, Harrap

Bridges, T. C., *The Book of Discovery*, Harrap

Brown, Harman, Jeanneret, *The Story of Canada*, Copp Clark

Campbell, Marjorie Wilkins, *The Nor'Westers*, Macmillan

Cordier and Robert, *History of Young America*, Rand McNally

Cordier and Robert, *History for the Beginner*, Rand McNally

Chafe, J. W., *Canada Your Country*, Ryerson

Coffman and Goodman, *Famous Explorers*, Dodd Mead

Cottler and Jaffe, *Map Makers*, Ryerson

Dalgleish, Alice, *America Begins*, Scribner's

Dickie, Donalda, *The Great Adventure*, Dent

Dickie and Palk, *Pages from Canada's Story*, Dent

Duvoisin, Roger, *They Put Out to Sea*, Knopf

Edwards, C. A. M., *Son of the Mohawks*, Ryerson

Finch, R., *Heroes of Discovery*, University of London Press

*Fiske, John, *The Discovery of America*, Vols. I and II, Houghton Mifflin

Gable, M. Harris, *Boys' Book of Exploration*, Dutton

*Heyerdahl, Thor, *The Kon-Tiki Expedition*, Allen and Unwin

Innes, M. Q., *Changing Canada*, Vols. I, II, Clarke, Irwin

Kamm, Josephine, *He Went with Captain Cook*, Harrap

Kates, Jerome S., *Minute Stories of Famous Explorers*, Grosset and Dunlap

Kidd, Kenneth, *Canadians of Long Ago*, Longmans Green

Knox, Olive, *Black Falcon*, Ryerson

Knox, Olive, *Little Giant*, Ryerson

---

*For the teacher.

*Lloyd, Christopher, *Captain Cook*, Faber and Faber
Lucas, Mary, *Vast Horizons*, Viking
Marshall, H. E., *Our Empire Story*, Nelson
Lambert, R. S., *North for Adventure*, McClelland and Stewart
Outhwaite, Leonard, *Unrolling the Map*, McClelland and Stewart
*Pohl, Frederick, *The Lost Discovery*, Norton
Pyne, Mable, *The Little History of The Wide World*, Houghton
  Mifflin
Pyle, Howard, *Book of Pirates*, Harper
*Stefansson, Viljhalmur, *Great Adventures and Explorations*, Dial
  Press
Syme, Ronald, *Henry Hudson*, Morrow
Synge, M. B. A., *A Book of Discovery*, Harrap
Tait, George E., *Famous Canadian Stories*, McClelland and Stewart
Tait, George E., *The World Was Wide*, Ryerson
*Van Loon, W. H., *The Story of the Pacific*, Harcourt Brace
Werner, Elsa Jane, *The Golden Geography*, Simon and Schuster
*Williamson, J. A., *Cook and the Opening of The Pacific*, Hodder
  and Stoughton
Makers of Canada Series, Oxford
Ryerson History Readers, Ryerson

SOME PICTURES TO LOOK AT

Voyage and Discovery, Informative Classroom Picture Series, Moyer
Life In Colonial America, Informative Classroom Picture Series,
  Moyer
Pioneer Days, Informative Classroom Picture Series, Moyer
Indian Life, Informative Classroom Picture Series, Moyer
Transportation, Informative Classroom Picture Series, Moyer
Man On Record, Informative Classroom Picture Series, Moyer
Collins, Alan C., *The Story of America In Pictures*, Doubleday
Jefferys, C. W., *The Picture Gallery of Canadian History*, Vols. I to
  III, Ryerson
Moore and McEwen, *A Picture History of Canada*, Nelson